Other books by Jim Andrews

Polishing God's Monuments: Pillars of Hope for Punishing Times

The Finality of Jesus Christ: Exploring the Many-Roads-To-God Myth

Dispatches from the Front Lines: Reflections on the Glory and Grind of Pastoral Ministry

A Life Worth Dying For

The Radical Meaning of Christian Excellence

Revised Edition

by

Jim Andrews

A Life Worth Dying For

ISBN 978-0-9891549-0-1

All inquiries should be addressed to: jwa575937@yahoo.com.
All scriptural citations, unless otherwise noted, are from the New American Standard Bible. The reader will often find within those citations bracketed words, phrases, etc. intended by the author to clarify the biblical text.

Printed in the United States of America

IN APPRECIATION

Several people helped with editing and proofreading this manuscript for whom I am most appreciative. My thanks to Lynne Mackey, Barbara Scherer and Jerri Barrett for their invaluable assistance on the first edition. I am also deeply appreciative of the editing skills of my sister, Jan Van Horn, who inherited many of the writing talents of her grandmother, Granny Deitz. Jan has produced the revised edition. For any residual errors I accept personal responsibility.

I also am grateful beyond words to Jimmy and Ivo Park for their invaluable assistance in bringing this book (and others) to publication. They are the embodiment of great abilities wrapped up in a godly, servant spirit.

Chapter 1

Revisiting Christian Excellence

"Nothing clears the mind, clarifies vision or resets values like an eternal perspective"

Like most books, this one has a history, but mine may be a little more tangled than most. This excellence motif has slowly evolved into the final shape it has taken in this volume. Some of us believers, I suppose, are just hardwired to aspire to transcend the average and to excel in what we do in the spirit of Ecclesiastes 9:10, "Whatever your hand finds to do, verily, do it with all your might." We don't necessarily need to be rich and famous . . . just to satisfy an inner imperative. "Small fry" though we may be in the larger scheme of things, we still yearn to rise above the surrounding mediocrity.

That is the target audience for this little book---believers endowed with a spirit that requires more of them than just drifting through life, going through the motions, never making a difference or leaving a wake. If your spirit is infused with the noble notion of excelling for Christ's sake in all the things that really matter, then this short volume is for you and your kind.

My interest in and passion for this theme goes back to the days when I was teaching in Bible college. Initially what stoked my fire was, not just my own native programming, but seeing in our student body some truly bright and talented students who, had they any ambition to excel, might have kicked a dent in something. Unfortunately, I soon discovered many (delightful as they otherwise may have been) lacked the drive for anything more than making the grade and moving on, to who knows where.

During that decade I had a number of students with the brains to perform at a high level at any university in the country. As the father of two girls, it especially grieved me to see some of these very smart and talented young women (who weren't preparing for vocational ministries) breezing their way through Bible college like academic catamarans in a favorable wind, and then, a whole ton of money later, graduating with a degree that qualified them to work at Denny's. Terrible waste! More than once, I told some of them that and urged them to bail, go get a marketable degree, and go out there in the world and show everybody what a savvy Christian woman could do. Sad to say, most of them were satisfied to hide out in the Bible-college cocoon, scout out a Christian mate and accomplish nothing worthy of their gifts.

Don't get me wrong here. This writer is the farthest thing from a feminist fellow traveler. I am *all for* Christian women devoting themselves to domestic life; I absolutely applaud it. What I am talking about are people with million-dollar minds bringing a 25-cent vision to the project of life. You see, some of these gals didn't opt for the domestic life out of vision; they settled for it for lack of one. *That* is what I personally deplore---no drive to transcend the ordinary. This directionless spirit of mediocrity is hardly in the mold of the noble housewife of Proverbs 31:10-31!

In response to my long-standing passion for this subject, I prepared for our students a couple of chapel lectures on this topic. With many, those lectures struck a nerve. Over the years students and colleagues urged me to publish them. As I set out eventually to amplify my topic to book length, a funny thing happened en route. As it turned out, this matter of excellence was trickier from a Christian perspective than I first realized. The more I pondered my subject, the more my conception of what "excellence" really means *for a Christian* morphed. For example, as much as I personally admire excellence in the usual categories in which humans typically strive to distinguish *themselves* (note that phrasing), my thinking evolved. I started to see that for a believer in Christ, pursuing those traditional forms of excellence fell way short of the biblical excellence God calls us to. That was a big shift for me.

You see, I for one had always been scandalized by mediocrity and ineptitude in Christian endeavors. From a youth, I always felt that we Christians needed to polish up our act, lest by lack of competence and class in the way we do things, we embarrass the name of Christ. And on that score, my mind hasn't changed a great deal. There indeed is something to be said for doing all things well.

Even so, I gradually came to realize that my original vision of excellence, as a Christian target, was too much in the mundane, temporal vein of pursuits that, in the final analysis, don't really matter *if detached from our higher goals as people of God.* As my thinking matured, a new model evolved of the shape Christian excellence ought to take. The revised version, I think, does not exclude the traditional, but transcends it by far in terms of goal and motivation.

Certainly, it is more biblically rooted and distinctively Christian than my initial, more secular conception of what the pursuit of excellence was all about. The more I reflected, I saw more clearly how misplaced my original emphasis was.

Not that my earlier standards and values were *all* wrong. Just that they were *too* wrong. Somewhere along the line, it began to dawn on me that when we talk about raising standards of excellence in the (institutional) church, what we typically have in view are not categories God would link with that attribute.

Gradually the light dawned. I began to see that the usual targets of our pursuits of excellence are not really *biblical* goals, but cultural brass rings that make no spiritual difference. In other words, my epiphany was this: Our Christian ideals don't always spring from *revelational imperatives,* but from merely *cultural benchmarks.* In the end, I realized that genuine *Christian* excellence is a *sui generis* (i.e., something in a class by itself). And the driver of the aspiration for pure Christian excellence is a biblical, not human, value system. Seeing that, well, the implications for the pursuit of excellence were sweeping.

So, a very long pause. I stopped to refine and overhaul my original thesis. This book is the fruit of that better vision. What I offer herein is, I believe, a distinctively Christian "philosophy" of excellence that better squares with our calling in Christ and directs our energies and abilities where they ought to be focused, rather than diverting them to the service of vain and unfruitful ends and endeavors.

And, the Christian vision, as I reframed it, is far superior to the traditional. Whereas the Scriptures call ordinary believers to true Christian excellence, the traditional approach invites exceptional persons to mere ordinary excellence. The Christian aspiration is cosmic in its vision; the traditional pursuit is merely cosmetic. The latter, as mentioned, is not necessarily excluded from the former, but the former is not usually included in the pursuit of the latter. And here is another crucial discovery along the way: To excel in a Christian way, we must, first and foremost, excel at the point of our primary identity, not our secondary vocations. We must resist falling into the trap, as most do, of letting our chosen professions---engineers, brokers, accountants, attorneys, techies, doctors, musicians, artists, writers, athletes, etc.---define who we really are at our core. Should we lapse into that error, that blurring of our identity will divert our quest for excellence into some (biblically) irrelevant veins. Whatever else we may be, we must bear in mind that, first and foremost, we are *Christians*---followers of Christ, i.e., disciples or learners of Jesus.

That is our primary and proudest identity. Unless we excel at that high point, any other marks of excellence we may achieve, in the eyes of God, are not worth the powder it would take to blow them up with. That is no overstatement. For the believer, this yardstick (excelling at simply being Christian) has to be the ultimate benchmark of excellence. Hence, the pursuit of excellence for Christians has little to do with charging out there like Olympians into this competitive world, getting all sweaty, and proving that whatever they can do, we can do as well or better. Those temporal skills and achievements may win kudos for us, but do they really bring any glory to God? Recognizing this faulty mental state substantially changes the whole equation of true excellence. My position, therefore, is that all human achievements and the accolades that go with them are nothing to get all jazzed about, except as those attainments truly *complement* our mission and *complete* our maturation in Christ.

In short, for believers to excel in tangential things but fall short in our spiritual calling---to be a disciple of Jesus Christ---is to miss the essential thing. And that, from a Christian perspective, would represent a gross surrender to the worst form of mediocrity, no matter how many ways we might excel in envied traditional categories.

And here, I think, is a most beautiful and compelling aspect of this more biblical vision of excellence---*the target lies totally within the reach of the earnest, but under-endowed believer. It is not elitist, but blessedly egalitarian. In the only way that really matters, the most ordinary Christian can be extraordinary. No one is excluded from the chase by the accidents of birth or circumstances, as is the case with most of the forms of excellence the world trumpets.*

There you have, in a nutshell, the perspective of this book. Bottom line, I insist that *the essence of excellence for believers is not being good at the things we do, but rather excelling at who we are in Christ.* There is a life worth dying for. Of course, these premises evoke some natural questions. These I have tried to anticipate and answer along the way.

Chapter 2

Rumblings of a Divine Discontent

"Is there a rumor in the soul that we are less than God meant us to be?"

"I want to make a difference."

"I hate mediocrity."

"I believe in doing things well or not doing them at all."

Sound familiar? Maybe like an echo? Like you, maybe?

Are you perchance one of those gifted, high-achieving, performance-driven Christians who likes to think of yourself as basically a winner? Does nature compel you to hit a home run whenever life sends you up to bat? With you, are high standards of performance both a matter of personal pride and Christian witness?

Or, to the contrary, maybe you may see yourself as so immutably average that any high hopes are deader than a graveyard at midnight. You think of yourself as being as boring as a doorknob . . . as undistinguished as a row house. No impressive resumé of accomplishments to your credit. No medals, no trophies, no ribbons, no clippings. None of those exceptional gifts or magical talents that beckon fame or call forth a torrent of accolades.

Long ago, you resigned your adolescent visions of celebrity and settled for reality. Divine providence, it appears, has destined you for a life of stubborn obscurity. Even so, your modest attainments and equipment notwithstanding, the truth is, underneath those unremarkable veneers, you are not so commonplace after all. Something about you drives you to do your best. Always has. *Even after* life rendered its irreversible verdict that you are not the best. Yet, for all that, something in you can't settle for being ordinary, even if you seem doomed to be average. For you there is a saving difference between the two. You can resign yourself to being average. What you can't settle for is a life that never gets beyond the ordinary. With *willful* mediocrity you can reach no agreement. Somehow, you want to break through and rise to that peculiar greatness reserved for little people who refuse to be small. There is, after all, an ordinary Christian who somehow exceeds himself and becomes extraordinary in those most important ways open to us all. This book is for folk like you especially.

Or, you maybe are one of those intense, idealistic Christians who is suddenly fed up . . . tired of the empty success games . . . bored with GQ yuppies and hollow status symbols . . . sick of worldly enterprise thinly disguised as a Christian exercise. You just want to cut the nonsense and to get back to spiritual basics. Your passion is simply to excel where it really counts---at being Christian. What pushes your buttons is the thought of going for broke and living recklessly for Jesus Christ. I call it *a life worth dying for*. You long to transcend the appalling spiritual mediocrity (if not outright hypocrisy) that marks so much of what passes for modern Christianity.

This book, I trust, has a special message for you too. Anyone who can resonate with the title of William

Law's classic, *A Serious Call to a Devout and Holy Life,* should find a starting point and some helpful direction in this volume.

That Gnawing Sense of Destiny Disappointed

Within many of us there is (or once was), I suspect, what one might term "a hangover" from the Adamic fall. It exists sometimes in the form of a thirst for greatness . . . or a vague restlessness with the status quo . . . or an internal nagging to transcend the tedium of the ordinary. Maybe all of the above. However one may describe it (or account for it), it's a hole in our spiritual psyche that I think of as a gnawing sense of destiny disappointed.

Part of that residual yearning for significance has, I imagine, its roots in the same psychological dynamic that evokes in a decaying society that familiar nostalgic yearning for the "good ole" days. Sooner or later every culture on the downslide seems to develop a sense of disappointed destiny. So begins that longing for the golden years and a wish to recapture its former hopes. Witness, for example, Tom Brokaw's onetime bestseller, *The Greatest Generation.* Implication? The best is behind us; how sad.

Is there perhaps a similar phenomenon at an individual level? Is there, universally ingrained in the human consciousness, a vague sense of melancholy, a rumor in the soul, so to speak, that we are less than we were . . . less than we ought to be . . . less than we could be . . . a sense of original destiny trashed? Maybe I'm all wrong, but I theorize there survives in many of us a subconscious residue of racial memory of shattered promise and brokenness. That subconscious "memory" may partially account for that relentless but generally futile struggle in many human beings to escape from the clutches of the ordinary.

Whatever it is, it persists in many of us and it doesn't yield to cheap solutions. Not even great achievement can satisfy the inner demand for something more fulfilling. Whatever is missing, the remedy hardly lies in great accomplishment, for the human quest for fulfillment and thirst for significance is elusive, even in the midst of trophies of worldly distinction.

Those of us whose lifework entails a bit more tracking of human behavior than some see it all the time: Successful people seem to live in the sun. Nevertheless, squalls of restlessness forever sneak up on their unprotected euphoria, soaking their spirits in despondency. Like starving humans trying to quell hunger and stave off death on a diet of lettuce from the city dump, the rich, the famous and the talented always, in the end, find their "harvest" unsatisfying. They fight each other for the "garbage" they use to fill that vacuum, which is created by the absence of God and the sustaining purpose that flows from His presence. It's a hole in their emotional pockets they can't fill, because the "filler" is unfulfilling. Little wonder our cultural heroes so commonly finish life out of the running, the pitiful slaves of drugs, drink, debauchery and discontent. I think of it as the "Elvis syndrome."

At home I have an old illustrated edition of Bunyan's *Pilgrim's Progress.* In it is a poignant but pitiful rendering of Bunyan's Muckraker. There in filthy, tattered rags, bowed miserably over his dirty rake, he stands hopelessly in muck up to his knees. Trouble is, the Muckraker never looks up. His vision is riveted right there. Yet, just inches above his head is a resplendent crown. If only he would just look up!

What I have described as a general human phenomenon takes a different form in the believer, however. If, in the world, there is this aforementioned *deformed* discontent that seeks relief in vanity, in the believer there is a *transformed* discontent born of the indwelling Spirit that finds relief and renewal in conformity to Christ . . . in honest discipleship. In the Christian, there is a *godly* impatience with all the undertow of the Fall. We long to transcend our foolishness, our pettiness, our blindness, our selfishness and our brokenness. Surely that divine discontent was in the mind of the Apostle Paul, who acknowledged it in these words:

> "We know that the whole creation has been groaning as in the pains of childbirth right up to the present time. Not only so but we ourselves, who have the first fruits of the Spirit, groan inwardly as we wait eagerly for our adoption as sons, the redemption of our bodies"
> (Romans 8:22-23).

That groaning within ourselves is a restless but devout longing to shake off the shackles of fleshly weakness and to put on the vestments of our final glory as sons of God. It is a transformed thirst of the royal family for true excellence, for escaping from the ordinary . . . for living up to our pedigree.

For a maturing Christian, this divine discontent is less a frustration than a source of inspiration. Though we have learned to respect the limitations imposed by our flesh-bound existence here, we see the possibilities unleashed by life in the Spirit. Not only do we discover the potentiality of His power through the Word, but we have also tasted its reality in ourselves and witnessed its transforming ability in others.

We have in our sights the crown of true greatness He dangles over the heads of His children. To claim it, we must refocus our values, redeploy our energies and resources, and resist unfruitful earthly pursuits. This ambition to please Him and to be conformed to Him is the blessed afterthought of our divine discontent with the status quo. Such a vision of excellence is not merely an alternative to the traditional pursuit, but also is an inner imperative for a child of God.

People in general have some sort of perverted genius for wasting their time on earth. Some just want to party and have fun (the hedonists). Some seem to exist for no higher purpose than to prove to themselves that they are actually alive (the thrill seekers). Not a few invest their whole existence apparently in making Mother Earth a cleaner, safer place to die (the environmentalists). Others expend themselves angling for the sweet taste of worldly power and influence (the politicians and activists). Of course, there is an underclass who are content to mark time just raising Hell and victimizing whomever is unfortunate enough to cross their path (the criminals). Some devote their self-righteous passion to chasing after vain utopian rainbows (the political left). Some live to reinstate an imaginary American past (the political right). Others are content just to make a bundle (the capitalists). Many just want to make a name for themselves (the performers). I can't speak for you, but personally I am dying to make a difference---a difference for Christ

On a recent vacation, my wife, Olsie, found a fascinating article in *National Geographic* magazine (March,

2011) about a 29-year-old extreme trekker who has earned quite a reputation for himself through his hiking conquests. A graduate of an elite university, then a Wall Street dropout, he lit out first on the famed Appalachian Trail, got the fever and has been conquering the wilds ever since.

Since 2002, having logged more than 25,000 miles on foot, he has survived and thrived under some of the most challenging and dangerous environmental conditions one could think of. As Olsie related the story to me and all the tortures he had endured over that span, the question leapt to my mind and shot out of my lips:

> "And for what?"
> Immediately she echoed it back to me,
> "Yes, and for what?"

At the end of the day what does any of it matter? I couldn't help but wonder if, out in the cold or tucked in his bed roll under some starry sky, the same question may not have occurred to him. You know, one can cuddle up to nature and caress her like a long-lost lover, as many these days delight to do, but in the end, let's face it: Nature will never return our love or our passion. In a sense, earth may be our mother, but certainly she is not God, even if to some fools she is a goddess. One day it's all over and we die and then what? What's the payback in terms of enduring value? Nothing. Absolutely nothing.

Oh, how human destiny is disappointed in our vanity and frivolity! No wonder there is a rumor of discontent in the soul. Such massive surrenders to mediocrity in terms of noble purposes!

Tracking down the roots of our massive cultural surrender to nothingness, in the name of something or other, is beyond the scope of this modest work. I would guess it is, in part, a slop-over effect of a fast-buck, mass-producing, throw-away culture with no sense of the absolute or the transcendent. Nothing lasts. Nothing is fixed. Nothing matters. Nothing (so the thinking goes) is beyond or above us. So why reach? Somehow, I would think, that matrix of sentiments has to be in the mix.

One thing I do know is this: There has been a horrendous slop-over effect of the culture in our churches. Mediocrity (and worse) reigns big time.

In order to raise our sensibilities to the scale of the problem and our consciousness to the scope of our general surrender to gross mediocrity, and, hopefully, to fire us with contempt for it and restless resolution to renounce it in favor of pursuing the radical meaning of Christian excellence, I now regretfully offer your Christian nostrils a strong whiff of the toxic smell of mediocrity in our churches.

Chapter 3

A Toxic Smell of Mediocrity

"Like toxic spills, the pollutions of the world eventually leak into the churches and contaminate their environments."

Sometime back I was in Denver for the funeral of a dear family friend. On the way to the interment, a pastor friend (and former student of mine) was discussing the cause of the spiritual derailment of the deceased's son, a highly successful project manager in the aerospace industry. "The thing that really threw him," he related sadly, "was the moral failure of so-and-so (his senior pastor back in his high school days). That made him cynical." I knew exactly who he was talking about and the whole shameful story.

My pastor friend went on to tell me, "You know, Jim, that was not the first time (of this man's moral failure). It turned out that the elders had been covering it up because some of them had their own moral transgressions to hide, so they were in no position to come down hard on him. There was just a whole culture of corruption in that church. That's what got to the boy."

Thereupon, I mentioned to him how shocked I had been years after the fact to receive a slick flyer from a megachurch in the Seattle area promoting a big Christian education conference in which one of the advertised representatives and speakers for one well-known publishing house was none other than this aforementioned disgraced pastor!

"Oh, Jim, you think that is bad. Let me tell you just how messed up things are. When they (the local church in Denver) were picking up the pieces, so-and-so (a guy we both knew and another former student of mine) was tasked to call all the groups that the (defrocked) pastor had been scheduled to speak for in the coming year or so. When he told them that the ousted pastor would have to cancel, many would press for more information, and, finally he would be forced to divulge that the cancellation was due to moral failure. Guess what many of them asked next? 'Well, when *will* he be available?'"

Oh, my! I was stunned at that. What a mentality in the church these days! Just like a hockey violation, a minute in the penalty box and then you can take to the ice again. Is it any wonder that the world mocks our hypocrisy?

Living in an environment pervaded with the spirit of mediocrity, it is not really surprising that we believers betray some of its symptoms, especially in the form of degraded moral standards. How hard it is to walk a muddy road without our shoes getting dirty. In our churches the spirit of mediocrity (to say the least) is frankly out of control.

Nowhere is our declension more glaring than on the spiritual front. The love of God is pervasively tepid, at least based on the evidentiary standard of John the Apostle (1 John 5:3). John declares to any who might mismeasure it by applying a certain matrix of devotional feelings or by confusing it with a hand-waving, teary-eyed, blissed-out look, that, on the contrary, "this is the love of God, that we keep His commandments and [in doing so] His commandments are not burdensome [or irksome]" (Brackets mine for clarity).

Today, any talk of "the fear of God" is viewed by some as almost pathological, a throwback to law, before grace was ushered in by Jesus Christ. Appetite for the Word of God has given way in our time to a generation that prefers a diet of psychobabble. Everywhere, pulpit chefs of the Dr. Feelgood variety test the wind and tickle the ear, all in uncanny accordance with the Apostle Paul's caveat to Timothy (2 Timothy 4:3). Our churches are filled with the kin of Salome's mother who still insist on having the head of any would-be John the Baptist on a platter. When I last checked, data available on the Internet revealed that as many as 1300-1700 pastors a month (!) were being discharged from their pulpits. Some of these were doubtless for incompetence, others for immorality, some for noncompliance (with the games people play), but not a few, I suspect, owing to intolerance for prophetic preaching.

Today, in many churches the pursuit of holiness seems as old-fashioned as pantaloons. By contrast, our favorite obsession seems the pursuit of emotional "wholeness." Not that the latter is an illegitimate goal; it just isn't the primary one. People just don't get it. The highway to Happiness runs directly through Holiness. But folk are always looking for a less radical and less stressful bypass. Yet, emotional wholeness without moral holiness is as impossible as physical health without nourishment. Even so, many church people and their pastors seem more interested in psychology than theology, in redemption by means of social legislation than by Gospel proclamation and in saving America than in rescuing lost souls in it.

The Missing Link

We Christians have not tended to link the quest for godliness with the pursuit of excellence. The burden of this book is to establish that link---not merely to show that this religious dimension is surely included in the concept, but that, for a Christian, it is the essence of it. This premise accounts for the spiritual and moral focus of this chapter on symptoms of mediocrity in the churches. As we develop our vision, it will become clearer why we downplay the pursuit of excellence in its more traditional associations.

Except for supernatural enablement, it would be ridiculous to live in the world and yet expect to live above it. However, the new birth makes the impossible possible.

> " . . . His divine power has granted us everything pertaining to life and godliness" (2 Peter 1:3).

Now persons deeply fallen can rise above the standards of the world and live on a transcendent plane, one that honors the God who purchased us with the precious blood of His unique Son. Drawing upon the resources of the Holy Spirit available to all those in organic union with Jesus Christ through faith, the most ordinary believer can be extraordinary and serve God with everlasting distinction.

The Gap between Potentiality and Reality

Call me blind, but I personally see little evidence that the average self-proclaimed Christian is taking dead aim on living up to his or her potential in Christ. We have been called to excellence but the pursuit of that calling, in most instances, doesn't appear too passionate or aggressive. My experience as both a teacher and a pastor has impressed this sad reality on me only too well. From what I have heard and observed, the typical believer is woefully remiss in practicing those spiritual disciplines so essential to spiritual growth and conformity to Christ. So far as I can tell, only a minority spends quality time in God's Word regularly. Most seem to pray very sporadically (usually in crisis situations). The average family has no compunction whatever about what I call "Sunday flight." Family time is valued more highly than God's time.

Recently, I missed a family in our church and wondered why I had not seen them since I returned from my summer vacation. On my birthday, I received a warm Facebook greeting, "Pastor Jim, hope you have a great birthday. We miss you." Gee, had they moved and no one told me? I responded: "So-and-so, thank you! Where are you?" No response. So I asked their care group leader what the deal was. "Oh, their children have Sunday sports now, so they can't come to church." You have to be kidding me! Have we so lost our bearings, our sense of the ultimately important, our sense of what our families really need that we would let Sunday sports replace Sunday church? Yes, indeed. With those priorities, I fear those parents will lose their children to the world, in part because mom and dad never fully left it. They have left some "hoofs" back in Egypt (Exodus 10:26).

I love sports, but not at the price of my children's souls. Why are we so clueless about what it means to follow Christ? How is it that in some there is so little aspiration to break out of the worldly pack and excel in walking with God? Little wonder the average Christian is almost a total stranger to heartfelt praise and worship, except for the kind artificially induced in skillfully manipulated mass settings where one "drafts" almost involuntarily on the mindless emotions of the herd. It evaporates as quickly as the crowd.

True, in some cases, the real explanation of that embarrassing gap between profession and performance is flat-out hypocrisy. As the New Testament teaches us, not everybody in church is in Christ. The faith that counts is in the heart, not on the lips. In short, what counts for faith today in many churches is little more than folk religion, not biblical religion. But more about this issue in another chapter.

In many instances, however, the problem is casual inconsistency. Owing to our infantile grasp of the glory of God and our gross ignorance of our vulnerability to the Enemy's deceptions, we sometimes don't pursue our mission and mandate as seriously or single-mindedly as a more mature understanding would dictate. Like reckless swimmers in the ocean surf, we ignore posted warnings of undertows because we underestimate the danger. In the same way, we believers wade in the waters of vicious riptides. Worldly waves threaten to suck us under and take us far out into the secular sea. Unless we are diligent to appropriate all our grace resources and to resist the secular tide with all our energies, we will inevitably wind up thrashing about in spiritual mediocrity. Accommodation to spiritual mediocrity in the churches, as I perceive it, narrows down to at least three crucial areas. These may be differentiated as: 1) laxity in living in the world, 2) laxity in leading the churches out of the world, and 3) laxity in learning about the warfare with the world. Of course, those categories are not mutually exclusive, but they embody sufficient distinction in this context to warrant separating them. Those three areas relate generally to what we are to be in Christ, what we are to do for Christ and what we should know in serving Christ. Let me now address these grave errors sequentially.

Laxity in Living

In this area let me flag the way we are seduced into moral mediocrity. That the sins of the world tend to become the sins of the Church is well known. Again, it is hard to live around dirt without getting dirty. Constant proximity tends to blunt our sensitivity. The repetition of an outrage will in time mellow the initial shock, just as doctors and nurses get inured to bloody messes. Eventually garments once rent in moral indignation begin to be stealthily retrieved and recycled as robes of smug sophistication. At that point, people try to pass off for intellectual enlightenment what is simply a hard case of moral vertigo.

Back when I was teaching in the Denver area, a student wife came for the mail in my office building. As she turned to leave, almost offhandedly she mentioned that, as she passed the cars parked outside, she had noticed a large rattlesnake slithering on the hot pavement between the vehicles there. How could she be so casual about a danger like that? Simply because she had grown up in Oklahoma where rattlesnakes littered the landscape. She had even hunted them for sport. To her a rattlesnake was no big deal any more . . . like a spider . . . something better disposed of but nothing to get exercised about.

As you can imagine, the rest of us viewed the matter more seriously. News that, to her, deserved no more notice than a tiresome infomercial was, to us, a news bulletin, a legitimate cause for concern and immediate action. Given her background, however, her passiveness was understandable. I repeat: Constant proximity tends to dull our sensitivity.

That incident is a metaphor of the way believers and the churches are lulled to sleep. By degrees, chronic exposure to a threat erodes the sense of danger and the shock diminishes with repetition. The best cure for gagging at goriness is gradual exposure to more gore. In a similar way our consciences are desensitized little by little. An early warning sign is the stage where we begin to make light of what once shocked us, as if our newfound tolerance or indulgence represented a higher stage of enlightenment. Confident that we are just more sophisticated, the truth may be that our moral senses are just benumbed. The revision of our moral sentiments, far from representing a great leap forward, may signal a dangerous step backward. How often our acquired acceptance of behaviors that once repelled us is celebrated in uncritical self-delusion as a triumph over legalism, prejudice or Victorian narrowness. More times than we might imagine, our newborn broad-mindedness is not a triumph, but a tragedy. We have embraced vice and scorned virtue. Called to be agents of moral change, we have become victims of cultural assimilation. Instead of serving as beacons of light, we have receded into the shadows, mere cultural clones reshaped in the moral image of the world about us. It is so easy to become too casual and laid back about evil. The more we see it, the less threatening---and the more normal---it seems to be.

The temptation and the pressure are always there to be less rigid . . . to be less "judgmental." After all, open-mindedness is "in"; narrowness is out. Who wants to be the party pooper, stinking up everybody's day? Who wants to be stigmatized as self-righteous, puritanical, pharisaical, holier-than-thou or legalistic? We go far out of our way to prove otherwise . . . way too far sometimes. The path of least resistance is to go along to get along. Under that kind of social duress, it is not surprising that many pull in their horns, and, under an avalanche of contrary opinion, relax their convictions before altering them altogether---not because of Scriptural warrant but because of social intimidation.

As we covet acceptance and the badge of "enlightenment," the world can more easily extort our moral capital because we are so terrorized by the thought of social isolation and ostracism. I think some of what drives this emerging church movement is that very thing. Part of its appeal to the young is that they tend to be so fastidious about keeping in the good graces of their peers, so afraid of taking any stance that might ostracize or marginalize them, in everything from dress to doctrine.

Somehow we must coax them to just get over it---to resist cultural cloning. Once we are maneuvered into this compromising posture, we are at the mercy of the moral drift. Before you know it, morality is turned on its ear. What once was good is now evil, and what once was evil is now defended as good. With that phenomenon the prophet Isaiah was all too familiar.

> "Woe to those who call evil good, and good evil; who substitute darkness for light and light for

> darkness; who substitute bitter for sweet, and sweet for bitter" (Isaiah 5:20).

Well, its ba-a-a-c-k! And so the cultural accommodation runs amok. Exaggerated? Then please explain why the word "purity" makes so many uncomfortable, striking them as prudish. How many single women don't care to advertise the fact that they are virgins? And what ever happened to the word "chastity"? How many younger men and women today would feel honored if their local media outlets described them as "patriots" or "law and order" types? Why is it that "straight" (in the sense of well-ordered) youth are considered by so many as "squares" and "bores" while wild and lawless ones are thought to be interesting and exciting? Things are turned on their head today.

The NBA San Antonio Spurs for about a 10-year period were the winningest team in professional basketball, and, by all accounts, one of the best balanced and most skillful ever put together. Yet, because their players weren't all inked up, running around looking like a freak show and showing up regularly on police blotters, they failed, for all their success, to capture the imagination of the hoops world. Go figure.

As far back as June 1985, *USA Today* reported that the U.S. Supreme Court in a certain case had put its moral imprimatur upon lust. Speaking for the majority, Justice Byron White argued that "healthy titillation" of sexual desire is a good thing. Nothing has changed for the better with respect to moral convictions. That tendency in our relativistic atmosphere to redefine "poison" is a phenomenon as old as mankind and one that stirred the indignation of the prophets of ancient Israel. Times may have changed, but not our tendencies.

In the last quarter of the 20th century, when I sensed the gay rights movement gaining traction, I also sensed a corresponding change in the public attitude toward this deviant sexual practice. Gradually, I watched the public mood shift from utter abhorrence to tepid tolerance, to today's ever-widening acceptance. As I observed that phenomenon and listened to the public dialogue and gay rationalizations of their perversion, I predicted to my wife that, before long, somebody would be justifying pedophilia by the same logic gays were using then to advance their cause. Within a year of that prophecy, a news article appeared in *Time* magazine (Jan. 17, 1983) doing just that! Any evil, including murder and genocide, can by constant repetition and rationalization, gain the moral sanction of society.

The memory of Hitler stands as eloquent testimony of that reality. And don't forget that much of the German Church stood by, either in silence or consent, while millions of Jews were led as lambs to the slaughter. (Read Eric Metaxas' biography, *Bonhoeffer: Pastor, Martyr, Prophet, Spy,* if you have any doubts.) Of course, these moral flip-flops occur subtly. We fake out the conscience with a name change. Instead of talking about sexual perversion, we sterilize the dialogue with language games. (It's not perversity, but, ah, just diversity!) We disguise the darkness with phony, euphemistic labels like "sexual preference." As one of my colleagues suggested, when our society, in its advancing moral decay, begins in earnest to justify pedophilia, it won't sanction it as "child abuse"; it will rationalize it perhaps in the euphemistic name of "family intimacy"!

Far out? How many consciences have made peace with abortion under the antiseptic labels of "family planning"? We must not be smug in our illusion of moral sophistication. It may be that our consciences won't register because the batteries are dead. The conscience is the watchdog of the soul. Maybe it has just barked itself out.

If hardening of the moral arteries is one symptom of acculturation, another is a preoccupation with self. This obsession, known as narcissism (as many of you already know), is named after the mythical Greek youth Narcissus who was afflicted with a consumptive self-love. Living in this obsessive society that consumes itself chasing after the elusive mirages of self-fulfillment, self-esteem and self-determination, contemporary believers are showing signs of serious environmental contamination.

For the last few decades or so, relational motifs have almost displaced vertical themes as the diet of the churches. If the shepherds are culpable for dispensing this junk food, the sheep are to blame for encouraging them to provide it. The suppliers are just responding to their appetite for it. Something is seriously amiss when pastors would rather talk incessantly about marriage and the family than about the Father, about success rather than the Savior, about self-enrichment rather than self-denial, about relationships rather than discipleship, about being happy rather than being holy, about loving self rather than loving God, about negative emotions rather than redemptive transactions, and about positive thinking rather than biblical faith. Oh, I can hardly stand it!

Am I suggesting that we ought to feast exclusively on the vertical realities and ignore the horizontal problems? Not at all. Certainly it is consistent with biblical precedent to instruct believers in the duties and obligations of marriage and child-rearing. If our domestic life has no integrity, our message will lack credibility. The glory of God obviously has a stake in any feature of our existence, which, wrongly managed, might tarnish the Gospel or compromise our viability as servants of God. Relationships are truly important. The Scriptures speak a great deal to those issues.

However, our relationship to God is paramount and foundational. Today we start at the wrong end of the relational equation. A person who gets his act together with God . . . who squares his outstanding accounts with God, will be in much better position to right relationships with those from whom he is alienated.

Where mediocrity in the form of narcissism impinges is when this interest in strictly horizontal themes betrays a self-serving and self-centered orientation, rooted in motives as earthborn as the world's. When we deflect the eternal and the vertical to pursue our own health, wealth and happiness in this temporal existence, that is sub-Christian. When believers substitute a passion to know themselves for a passion to know God, put harmonious and fulfilling relationships with others ahead of seeking a harmonious and fulfilling communion with the living Christ, this is sub-Christian. It reflects a culpable indifference *to* and disregard *for* our calling.

The narcissistic orientation obsesses about issues of personal happiness; a theistic mentality focuses on the pursuit of godliness. Like a buzzard, the self-centered man scavenges the rotting remnants of vanity in search of self-enhancement. On the other hand, the Christ-centered person consents like a soldier to self-denial for the glory of God.

This myopic pursuit of happiness, therefore, represents a concession to paganism and is, for that reason, a capitulation to spiritual mediocrity, i.e., indifference to the standards appropriate to our high calling in Christ. Excellence requires that we distance ourselves from this worldly attitude, saturating our hearts with the Word of God and fixing our affections on things above. We have no choice but to live in the world. We can however choose not to be like it. That option requires a reordering of our agenda. Instead of squandering our energies in the quest for health, wealth and happiness, we must commit our energies and resources to the goals of holiness and the knowledge of God.

Another example of carelessness in personal living is our complacency about personal growth. I am not surprised that many of us are deeply flawed. What amazes me is how reluctant we are to admit our shortfalls and take appropriate steps to rectify them. There is far too much faking it. We are too gratified to be "right"' in style; too content to be dead wrong in substance.

For example, do we ever secretly congratulate ourselves for superior form even as we harbor venomous feelings? Can we deny that sometimes with us "bad press" is a greater fear than a bad conscience? Do we sometimes exert more effort to keep from looking bad than to keep from being bad? In other words, is it more important not to appear unspiritual than to be spiritual? Woe to us when we are more attentive to our public image than our private integrity!

It's so easy in the pew to pass window dressing off as interior decorating . . . so easy in fact that many of us are satisfied when this kind of mediocrity passes for maturity. Unfortunately Christian leaders too often are role models for this form of dissimulation. It is easier to sweep our dirt under the rug than out of our hearts.

Pastoring becomes posturing. We are untouchable . . . and unconscionably complacent. Familiarity with the holy has bred contempt. We have become comfortable with our diseases and are proud of our adjustment to our infirmities. And the sheep follow suit.

Is the distinction lost on us altogether between a pious surface and a proper spirit, between putting up a good fight and putting on a good front? Too long we have watered our horse at the trough of pious platitudes in the comfortable valley of Mediocrity. Let us get on to the high ground of pious attitudes where Excellence dwells.

Laxity in Leading

Individual laxity in living, like adolescent misbehavior, is constantly being encouraged by laxity in leadership. For example, I personally am amazed by our tolerance of moral and ethical derelicts in our churches.

Let's face it: The response of the average evangelical church to blatant sin typically ranges somewhere between craven tolerance to frozen indifference. Our sufferance of brazen libertines and ethical outlaws is both appalling and pervasive. Rare indeed is the modern church (or parachurch organization) that has the pure conscience, the moral fortitude and the godly zeal to declare war on aggravated sin in its own house. The spirit of Phinehas (Num. 25:6-8) is deader than a stump in modern church life.

One evening in my late night channel surfing, I came across a supposedly Christian TV channel. Up there in the spotlight, beamed around the world (unfortunately), was a high profile musician who had recently been mired in an adulterous affair. But there he was, bold as brass. The whole supporting cast had the brow of a harlot. None of them knew how to be ashamed. You see (we seem to have forgotten), before forgiveness comes repentance. Spurgeon once said that such people ought not be admitted back into visibility until their repentance was as notorious as their sin. Unfortunately, this is just one example of this kind of indifference to credibility and moral standards in our churches.

One of my acquaintances is a Dove award-winning Christian music artist. His wife is a good friend and former student of mine. For years she had told me (she only confirmed what I already suspected) that the whole "Christian" music scene is rotten to the bone and accountable to none. But who cares? People still buy their music and run over top of one another to hear them, especially the young. Who cares . . . God is gracious. (I think they have confused the term with *indulgent.*) Our churches today are so wimpy. It's always safer to pick on the heathen in the world than the pagans in the pew. It's easier to take on abortionists at some family planning clinic than adulterers in the congregation. How can we campaign so righteously against godless policies and two-faced politicians in government while giving refuge and comfort to big-bucks businessmen who make a mockery of the Gospel, cheating customers, exploiting employees and engaging in unethical business practices that would make a robber baron blush?

How low have our ethical and professional standards sunk when many Christians are more afraid of business dealings with other Christians than with the world? You don't know how many times I have heard fellow believers express that very sentiment. In a church

I once attended, there was an insurance man who was well-known (he was his own best cheerleader) for his tithing and evangelistic zeal. In that particular church, those virtues were certified seals of righteousness. No matter that this "brother" was financially irresponsible, owing everybody for miles around and forever fending off fate with lies and promises, the church elevated him to its official board. Does that make sense? Yet I could point to many similar examples, some with considerably less excuse than this.

Some years ago, the pastor of a large evangelical church related to me an incident that allegedly occurred in a Bay Area (California) church. A pastor had been having an affair (or affairs) and was unceremoniously exposed. The following Sunday he made a tearful confession and professed repentance, complete with the sackcloth and ashes routine. Then he tendered his resignation. The Board asked the congregation to remain while it officially convened to consider the matter. Shortly they emerged with their verdict. So impressed they were with the pastor's apparent contrition, they refused to accept his resignation! That outrage was second only to their subsequent decision to offer him a substantial raise as a token of their goodwill! I always wondered what they were trying to forgive *themselves* of.

Forgiveness is indeed appropriate where there is real evidence of repentance. But we have really missed the point when we fail to distinguish between restoration to fellowship and reinstatement into a sacred office. Our blindness in such matters is a testimonial to our growing indifference (in leadership) to biblical standards---the grossest form of Christian mediocrity.

As extreme as that case may sound, scenarios like that are not as exceptional as you may hope. Sadly they are on the rise. Jack Smith (a pseudonym) was the chairman of the Board of Deacons in his local Baptist church . . . a natural leader and seemingly a spiritual man. He had personally led the fight to have his church disaffiliate from its denomination because of its pervasive theological apostasy. Shortly thereafter his lovely wife succumbed to cancer. The church family rallied around him. Among his comforters in his ordeal was a next-door lady who, along with her husband, was also a member of the same church. Everything began sincerely. Mary (a pseudonym) helped with all those domestic things that most men are unaccustomed to. However, as is always the danger in such circumstances, what was born in Christian compassion drifted from its moral moorings out into the high seas of romantic feeling. Soon there were rumors as rampant as they were shocking. The man was a rock and nobody could believe he had a moral crack. Tragically all the smoke shortly revealed a fire. Mary filed for divorce. Bill (a pseudonym), her shattered husband, hoping that it would pass and that he could eventually regain her estranged affections, stayed in the church. However, his hopes were cruelly dashed when the couple, her divorce now finalized, were married.

Jack attempted to "sanitize" the whole affair by stepping down as Board chairman just prior to the marriage. As unconscionable as it had been for the church to stand by idly as he escorted Bill's estranged wife to services each Sunday, the most incredible episode in this ecclesiastical soap opera was yet to come. When Jack and Mary returned from their honeymoon, would you believe that on their first Sunday back, some of the congregation, as poor Bill sat by in bewildered silence, gave them a standing welcome! Not only that, but worse yet, they actually vied with one another for the honor of their company. How tolerance eventually gives way to acceptance and compromise gives birth to complicity!

Author William J. Bennett *(The Death of Outrage)* has talked about it in the culture. I am talking about it in our churches. What has happened to righteous indignation in the churches? Where is our sense of prophetic outrage when people who profess to know Christ thumb their noses at biblical imperatives, while cloaking themselves in pious clichés and a smokescreen of religious involvements? And what is wrong with us when we let sin destroy the foundations rather than risk a fire in the pews?

What minions of mediocrity we have become! Where is the *leadership?* What moral wimps we are! Over my long years I have heard pastors intone about taking over a church and blessing it with a so-called "healing ministry." Nothing wrong there, except that in my experience, this generally means sweeping under the rug all the sin that preceded it rather than confronting it. The "cure" only aggravates the disease. We don't need limp rags, but conscientious leaders. Of course, it is totally right to minister, figuratively speaking, to the lame, the halt, the sick and the blind---provided one does not do it like a pussy willow.

A true healing ministry is not one that will comfort people in their sin, but confront them with their sin and turn them from it. "Comfort the afflicted; afflict the comfortable." There's the balance. We must balance a posture of humility, knowing our own vulnerability, with a zeal for purity, knowing God's purpose and provision for the redeemed.

A woman in Denver once gave me a revealing explanation of the way one of these non-confrontational, so-called "healing ministries" had unwittingly helped her rationalize a biblically unsanctioned divorce. She and her husband had been Christians only briefly. When his social personality didn't change as she anticipated, she began to toy with the idea of divorce. That option became more appealing and viable to her because of the climate in this uncritically "accepting" church. For, within her short time in that body, Ann had witnessed a number of marital breakups, some with no biblical grounds whatever. Despite that, there was no discipline or censure at any level. She saw that any and all divorce was countenanced with no formal consequences. Encouraged by that laxity, she decided to extricate herself from an unfulfilling marriage.

If that is a ministry of healing, may God deliver us from such cruel healing! Something is wrong in a church when the climate incites rather than inhibits evil---and in the name of Christian love and mercy. We have confused mercy with indulgence and love with license. In our reckless, self-confident disregard of biblical standards in matters of morals, ethics and church discipline, we are functionally destroying the very lives we profess to be saving. Being so wise, we have become fools.

One of the hallmarks of a mature church is "speaking the truth in love" (Ephesians 4:15). The right pillar of the Church is charity; the left is veracity. To minimize either creates a heretical imbalance. Yet some boast in one at the expense of the other. The fallacy in this is the illusion that one can exist without the other. The fact is, love without truth is mere sentimentalism, and truth without love is mere scholasticism. Alone, one is as deadly as the other.

Unfortunately illustrations like these are not as exceptional as we would hope. I could multiply them from my own experience with tiresome redundancy. You no doubt could furnish a depressing litany of your own examples of moral and ethical laxity in our churches. Were we only talking about isolated cases, we might comfort ourselves with the hope that the disease is local and not systemic. However the range and recurrence of such incidents belie that illusion.

With maddening frequency, reports filter in from everywhere of believers ensnared in adultery, homosexuality and other forms of illicit sexual conduct. There is child abuse, domestic neglect, avoidable divorce, financial delinquency and blatant dishonesty. It is not uncommon for Christian employees to take advantage of employers; nor is it unknown for Christian employers to exploit employees, to disdain the poor and the defenseless, to fawn after the rich and influential and to wield power like a serpent rather than a servant.

Where is the leadership? None of this is new. From the beginning, the community of faith has been riddled with spiritual frauds, failures, faux pas and foibles. What generation has not suffered the disgraceful likes of biblical types such as Ham, Korah, Dathan, Achan, Balaam, Judas, Demas, Simon the sorcerer, Ananias and his wife, Sapphira, Hymenaeus and Alexander, and Diotrephes? The Enemy always recycles the toxic types of yesterday and lays the same traps for the people of God that have proved so effective in the past.

No one should be surprised if today, as well as tomorrow, the faith is scandalized by the embarrassing lapses of our Samsons, Davids, Solomons, Peters and Marks. All these sorts of failures are inevitable, but the point is, we should never allow them to be acceptable. We must never allow ourselves to become so immersed in our culture or wedded to its values that we become deeply conditioned by it or blasé about it. Holy indignation is in order, not carnal indifference.

Laxity in Learning

Here is a third major symptom of spiritual mediocrity in modern church life. In his little volume, *Your Mind Matters*, the late John R.W. Stott has observed that "the spirit of anti-intellectualism is prevalent today." That point has been resoundingly made by others, most notably in the 1990's by church historian Mark Noll in his *The Scandal of the Evangelical Mind.* Though I take issue with Noll's accommodation tendencies at some points, in general he is right.

What kind of person is anti-intellectual? *The Random House Dictionary of the English Language* defines an anti-intellectual as "a person who believes that intellect and reason are less important than actions and emotions in solving problems and understanding reality." In Stott, fortunately, we have a positive pastoral example (among others) in an evangelical world suffering from a serious case of brain cramp in the pulpit.

How does this anti-intellectual tilt reveal itself in our religious context? In its evangelical forms, anti-intellectualism has at least two manifestations, both of which obstruct our ability to build bridges to the secular city and to penetrate it with the transforming power of the truth (though one must acknowledge the sovereignty of God in the equation also). One aspect Stott pinpoints is a generous disdain for learning, combined with scoffing at any need for serious intellectual endeavor:

> “Many have zeal without knowledge, enthusiasm without enlightenment. In more modern jargon, they are keen but clueless. Now I thank God for zeal. Heaven forbid that knowledge without zeal should replace zeal without knowledge! God’s purpose is both, zeal directed by knowledge, knowledge fired with zeal. As I once heard Dr. John McKay say, when he was President of Princeton Seminary, ‘Commitment without reflection is fanaticism in action. But reflection without commitment is the paralysis of all action.’”

Stott’s comments are on the button. Let us not polarize knowledge and zeal, learning and loving, pietism and intellectualism, pragmatism and academics, as if those pairs represented alternative strategies for discharging our Christian mandate. We concur with him that in no way is an "arid, hyper-intellectualism . . . a dry, humorless, academic Christianity" superior to the "superficial anti-intellectualism" or vice versa. One extreme is as lamentable as the other. Willful stupidity is as dishonorable as woeful sterility. Both represent serious aberrations from biblical models.

Who among the prophets or apostles was distinguished for ignorance? The fact that the Scriptures do not exalt knowledge does not mean its writers despised it. In fact Jesus and the Apostles evinced it, much to the consternation of their adversaries, who could not, given their lack of formal education, account for their intellectual acuity and confidence. We must not confuse their educational disadvantages with learning deficiencies. Most of the servants of God in biblical history, so far as I can tell, were savvy, if not savants, in their time. None that I am aware of were empty headed.

All the inspiration in the world is no substitute for information. On the other hand, without the wings of inspiration, information seldom gets off the ground. To use maritime imagery, inspiration is related to the Christian voyage as the winds that drive the sails; information is the ballast that gives the vessel stability on its course. Therefore excellence does not leave us the option of choosing between loving and learning, between doing and thinking, between emotion and reflection, and between spirituality and scholarship. To ignore one at the expense of the other is to jeopardize the entire mission.

Other than a revival of moral integrity among evangelicals and a corresponding renewal of commitment to biblical authority, not only in faith but also practice, I think our second greatest need is a re-linkage of spirituality and scholarship, of content and commitment, of enthusiasm and intelligence. Somewhere we must get past the idea that those couplings are incompatible.

I remember a long ago conversation with Dr. Bruce Waltke around a banquet table one evening. He told me, "Jim, we need a new marriage between scholarship and piety." Yes, indeed. Dr. Bruce Ware, a friend of mine and former colleague, now a theologian at Southern Seminary, has echoed the same thing. In generations past, some of the most learned men of the

Church were also some of its most spiritual, some of its most informed were its most inspired. Take John Wesley, for example. Robert Mounce writes:

> "We usually think of John Wesley as an ardent evangelist. Travelling 5,000 miles per year on horseback, he preached over 42,000 sermons---an average of three a day. But in addition, he wrote more than 200 books and edited over 450 publications. He could quote the Greek New Testament more exactly than the English Bible. As a don at Lincoln College, Oxford, he taught logic and also classics in the original Greek and Latin."

After reading Bishop J.C. Ryle's *Christian Leaders of the Eighteenth Century,* I told my pastoral staff one Monday morning I felt like an ant in the shadow of elephants. My, how far we have fallen off the pace! Every era of church history bears witness to the fact that ill-equipped leadership is not a modern phenomenon. But has there ever been a time when educational opportunities were so bountiful and lack of learning so inexcusable? Yet, despite the extreme disadvantages of previous generations, it seems to me that in some periods at least, spiritual men of intellectual breadth and depth were more commonplace in the Church than today.

Perhaps it is for that very reason that Wesley is not remembered primarily as an intellectual man, though today even most seminary professors would be featherweights by comparison. Even an evangelist like George Whitefield was far more of a thinker and scholar than his modern counterparts. He was very accomplished in Greek and read widely. Luther and Calvin also stick out as great models of this marriage of scholarship and spirituality. At age 27, Calvin could write the first draft of his great *Institutes*. Today the average evangelical minister has not even read the *Institutes*!

In those days, there were a lot of giants on the earth; today there are mostly midgets. For all their massive learning, those great men did not neglect their spiritual cultivation. Holding spirituality and intellectuality in a complementary tension, they cut a swath for Christ like few before or since. We may not possess their capacious endowments, but we should in this respect resolve to emulate their vigorous investment.

Anti-intellectualism also appears when one turns his or her back on all the learning in the (secular) world because he equates it all with "the things of the world" and therefore of no value whatever. The fallacy here is the failure to distinguish the things that belong to our humanity from those that belong to our *fallen* humanity. Faltering at that distinction, some throw out the baby with the bath, confusing moral separation with social and intellectual isolation. Such a posture is reactionary, not revolutionary. It is defensive, not aggressive. It succeeds better in removing the Church from the world than in removing the world from the churches.

Instead of seeing the Scripture as the ultimate canon of true knowledge, the reactionary mentality misconstrues it as a rival to other knowledge when in fact, in God's common grace, the learning of worldly sages may in some instances confirm and complement the revelation of God. Christians (or at least they used to) take just pride in being a people of the Book.

However, it does us little credit to be a people of **only one** book---in the sense that we find no wisdom or value in any learning except what may be gained from the Scriptures. All truth is God's truth, even if that truth turns up in some garbage.

The price we pay for anti-intellectualism is high. The chickens do come home to roost. In capitulating to this form of mediocrity, many Christians lack the "intelligence" to operate effectively behind "enemy lines" or at high levels of cultural engagement. James Davison Hunter has pointed out this deficiency in his book, *To Change the World.* We are too ignorant of the opposition and what inspires it. Even if we had the answers, we wouldn't know the questions. Overstated? Maybe, but in my view, not by much.

There was a time when the Church could look to its leaders for intellectual leadership as well as for spiritual models. Cotton Mather and Jonathan Edwards come to mind. Today that is not so common. Pastors too often are nurses, not physicians; cheerleaders, not coaches; managers, not thinkers; promoters, not pundits.

May God give us thinking men with great hearts, but deliver us from midgets with small minds. May God give us men who are as vigorous in reflection as in action, and as distinguished for perception as for passion. May God deliver the Church from the admiration of one-sided deformity, whether in the direction of a thoughtless activism or a vacuous emotionalism or sterile intellectualism. May we be what we ought to be, do what we ought to do, and, by all means, know what we ought to know---and be incurably restless with any deficit.

The scene we have painted is not a pretty picture. Individually of course we cannot change it, though great fires have been ignited by a few sparks. But without any grandiosity, what we all can do by the grace of God is be real, hard-nosed disciples who are going for the gold rather than more churchy dilettantes who are along for the ride.

At this point, before we start talking in more expanded terms about what going for the gold looks like "on Monday morning," it is time for a little preliminary self-assessment. Before we take this trip, let us make quite certain that our heads and hearts are truly in the game.

Chapter 4

Playing a Game or in the Game?

"For just as the body without the spirit is dead, so also faith without works is dead" (James 2:26).

Years ago in my Denver days, out of the blue, a very uptown-looking gentleman popped unannounced into my office at the college where I was teaching. I do not recollect specifically what brought him my way. As we got acquainted, it turned out that this very handsome man, probably in his late 30's, was, that year, Denver's number-one residential real estate broker and a professing Christian who could "talk the talk" with any preacher in the western United States.

He told me he was a divorced father of three young boys, if I recall correctly. I got the impression he was a doting dad and a thoroughly committed Christian. Man, I was taken with him. This guy seemed to be the real deal, at least until midway in our talk. As he got more comfortable with me, he became more revealing. What struck me was his nonchalant manner of relating to me, with no detectable guilt, his lifestyle as a serial fornicator. It seemed he was bedding a different woman every other night

The revelation of his casual sex liaisons was no bigger deal to him than if he had mentioned offhandedly that, as motorists go, he had a heavy foot.

And that habit was not even what he came to talk about! It blew me away.

After that I shifted gears from admiration to admonishment. I took him to 1 Corinthians 6:9-10, Ephesians 5:5-7, Galatians 6:7-8, 1 John 3:7-10 and others, to warn him that, given his immoral lifestyle, he may be kidding himself about the integrity of his faith. Maybe God in his mercy, I said, had brought me into his life to be "a prophet," to rebuke his gross sin and turn him from immoral ways that spoke against an honest faith, or perhaps, I allowed, "you are just another make-believer who confuses presumption with conviction and one who needs a serious wake-up call." But as things stood, I told him, he was in danger of deceiving himself. He was not pursuing excellence in Christ, but excess.

Unfortunately, I could go on with scenarios like that *ad nauseam*.

As we consider a life worth dying for and the radical meaning of Christian excellence, this is a good place to take inventory. Are we the real deal or just religious bags of gas? Are we playing a game or in the game?

This 21st century promises to be full of testing times. A shake-out is probably on its way sooner rather than later. It's time for each of us to decide with clarity whether we're in the battle or just in the pew, in the stands or on the field. It's time to leave no doubt as we strive with excellence for the goal, "pressing on . . . for the prize of the upward call of God in Christ Jesus." (Philippians 3:14) Granted, none of us has "arrived" by any means, but it's time for all of us to be resolute in the pursuit of Christian excellence, "reaching forward to what lies ahead" (Philippians 3:13). It is time, in the adapted words of the Apostle Paul, "in view of the surpassing value of knowing Christ Jesus [our] Lord, to [be willing to] suffer the loss of all things, and count them but rubbish in order that [we] may gain Christ" (Philippians 3:8).

If indeed we are serious about following Christ into the radical meaning of Christian excellence, let us make up our minds to be done with half measures, to pull out the stops and get after it. Let us aim to distance ourselves from those either nominal or lukewarm Laodicean "Christians" whose hearts are barely in the game and whose so-called "faith" is not up for following. Let us make our calling and election sure (2 Peter 1:10) and refuse to be the kind of posturer decried by our Lord and the ancient prophets:

> "This people honors Me with their lips, but their heart is far away from Me" (Matthew 15:8).

And, in the process, let us emphatically reject the caricatures of Christian faith so pervasive in our church culture that nurture presumption and give the faith a bad odor. In my sights particularly are those in the evangelical tradition who are sucked into antinomian-like notions of cheap grace that teach, in effect (with some exaggeration on my part), that we believers can expect Heaven while we continue to live like Hell---that one can have his cake and eat it too.

The Scriptures know nothing of such a damnable doctrine. See 1 John 3:4-10 for confirmation on that. As long as people buy into this teaching, it allows them to be casual about their old carnal habits and worldly affections. There is no moral urgency about parting with such ways. It has the effect of blunting much of their spiritual incentive for pursuing full surrender to Christ the Lord. "The firm foundation of God stands, having this seal, 'The Lord knows those that are His,' and 'Let everyone who names the name of the Lord abstain from wickedness'" (2 Timothy 2:19). If that moral imperative is not etched on the heart of a saint, in all probability, the "saint" is an "ain't." Let us come to terms with this: There is, out there in our churches, a "faith" unworthy of the name. It is a caricature of biblical faith. There is what one might term a hollow faith as opposed to a follow faith. The latter has legs, the former only lips. Our pews are liberally sprinkled with the former, and it is a serial killer . . . a bogus faith that Christ will roundly disown when He returns. As He himself warned, Jesus will declare:

> "I never knew you. Depart from Me, you who practice lawlessness" (Matthew 7:23).

Saving faith follows Christ. It is suffused with a dying (to self) faith that lives and works through love (Galatians 5:6).

Just a couple of days after Denver's Tim Tebow's sensational 80-yard touchdown pass just 11 seconds into the overtime 2012 NFL playoff game that sunk the mighty Pittsburgh Steelers, there was chatter all over the internet about Tebow's Christian faith and his habit, in his collegiate days, of wearing under-eye patches (prohibited by the NFL) inscribed with "John 3:16."

A day or so afterward, an internet blog writer mentioned a University of Florida alum who touted himself as "a fellow Christian." When this man had seen Tebow in his collegiate days wearing that patch, he had looked up that Bible verse to see what it said.

Without mentioning that self-descriptive quote, I showed the blog to my wife, who likes Tim Tebow. That comment jumped off the page at her the same way it had struck me. In microcosm it said about all one needs to know about the contemporary state of the Christian "faith" in America, in particular. I mean, how does one explain a "fellow Christian" who is ignorant of John 3:16, for crying out loud? It borders on fantasy (at least to me) to believe that one who has received Jesus Christ as his Redeemer would be clueless about perhaps the most famous gospel verse in the New Testament!

That brought to mind a comment I had heard earlier, as I was getting ready for work one morning. A TV talking head declared all-knowingly that "90 percent of Americans identify themselves as Christians." Talk about a statistic that drastically dumbs down what it means to be a Christian! Though I doubt that fellow had any statistical basis for that claim, about this I have little doubt: Far more people in our churches profess the Christian faith than actually possess it. My basis for that assertion is partly Scriptural and partly experiential---an appalling gap between walk and talk, belief and behavior.

The truth is, in the race of faith (as the Bible makes abundantly clear), there are always in every generation contenders and pretenders, believers and make-believers, those who are just members of churches and those who are truly members of Christ. All may seat their fannies in the same pews but their hearts are by no means on the same page. We all just need to look ourselves honestly in the mirror and make sure that we are following Christ, not just faking it. Biblical faith, folks, is radical, not casual.

Oh yes, I agree totally, one's faith can be seminal (like a child's) and need time and nurture to grow fully into its suit. However, if it is genuine, grow it does under the nurturing and disciplining influence of the Spirit of God working through the Word of God (John 17:17). Sanctification follows justification as surely as the sun rises in the morning. In short, in the end, it finds its way home.

Now here's a big time peril. Some Christians are totally content with the supposed integrity of their faith, but actually quite casual about the obedience that should follow from it. What makes them rather cavalier about that is their notion that the root (faith) can actually exist in good order without the fruit (obedience) to prove it. Despite James' 2:26 explicit words to the contrary, they persist in this belief.

Many have been taught that to believe otherwise is to venture into legalism, mixing faith and works. And we know legalism is wrong, because "by grace we are saved through faith (alone)" (Ephesians 2:8). So, some of them keep going merrily along to church, doing all the churchy things and boasting of their faith in Jesus, while selectively ignoring His commands and living not a whole lot differently than the world. In short, for these folk (and there are a multitude of them), excellence in the form of obedience is not at all a morally compelling agenda.

To put it in its crassest form, many of these folk feel fortunate that, in Christ, they have a get-out-of-jail-free card where the prospect of judgment is concerned plus a paid-in-full reservation in Heaven. Now, if they like, they can have their cake and eat it too.

Perverse! Grace reduced to a Protestant form of indulgence. Sure, the gospel invites us sinners to come to Christ just as we are. But these folk assume salvation by grace gives them license to remain, if they want, pretty much as they were. In their grace model, divine justification is essential; divine sanctification is optional. Have it your way.

Just how wrong-headed this notion is we see in Luke 8:19-20, where the Lord Jesus made it so obvious. On that occasion it was reported to the Savior that "Your mother and your brothers are standing outside, wishing to see You." Seizing upon that teachable moment, Jesus made it clear as crystal that a relationship with Him was not based upon blood, but rather upon doing the will of God (i.e., faith-driven obedience). Said He, looking around at His disciples among the crowd:

> "My mother and my brothers are these who hear the word of God and do it."

If that is not clear enough about Jesus' view of the indissoluble connection between faith and obedience as we find it in James, it is inescapable in Luke 11:27-28, where, as the Lord was speaking, an approving voice from one of the women in the crowd bellowed out:

> "Blessed is the womb that bore You, and the breasts at which You nursed."
>
> Jesus swiftly corrected her:
>
> "On the contrary, blessed are those who hear the word of God, and observe it."

He was not talking about legal works as a condition of salvation, but faith-driven obedience, the latter being the fruit of which the former is the root. This was not a performance-based beatitude, but the performance-tested kind. Big difference.

The same relationship between faith and its natural complement is plain as day in our Lord's analogy (Matthew 7:24-27) between those who build an indestructible house upon the rock and those who build their failed house upon the sand. The difference between the two outcomes: The former is the wise man who hears "these words of Mine and acts upon them," whereas the latter (the foolish man) is "everyone who hears these words of Mine and does not act upon them."

No, the word "faith" is never used, but the logic is transparent. Faith and obedience (that is its natural reflex) are just flip sides of the same spiritual coin. It is only in the grip of that kind of faith---true, saving faith---that one finds a life worth dying for. Anything less is an imposter. Any other "faith" is unworthy of the name.

Believing in Christ and following Christ---it's the same difference. Faith says, "I will follow Jesus . . ." Following says, ". . . because I believe in Jesus." Again, two sides of the same coin.

Living faith . . . real faith . . . the faith that saves is a blue-collar faith. It is a faith that shows up in work clothes. Dead faith, the kind James talks about, just talks. Living faith walks the talk. Jesus Himself said it:

> "My sheep hear My voice and they follow Me" (John 10:27).

Sheep that don't follow aren't His flock. They don't follow Him because at bottom they don't really trust in Him. Believers follow and followers believe. Now, I must be very clear here: Are we suggesting a salvation based on faith plus performance? No way. We are saying the reality of faith is tested or verified by performance (following Christ). Real faith is a faith that works . . . a faith that responds to Christ the Lord . . . a faith that is alive to the Spirit and operates through love (Galatians 5:6).

Salvation, I stoutly affirm, is by God's grace through faith in Christ---and faith alone. We cannot earn salvation. We cannot even contribute to it. Not by meritorious performance. Not by rite nor ceremony nor sacrament. Not by affiliation with some religious institution. Yes, absolutely, salvation is "by grace through faith . . . not by works" (Ephesians 2:8-10).

And let no one read any undertones of spiritual perfectionism into my theology. None of us is remotely a sin-free zone. We believers are not immune to failure. Just like babies, we disciples must grow in understanding and develop strength of faith. Migration to spiritual adulthood is a sometimes fitful, painful and frustrating process. Maturity in Christ takes time, but it is not the habit of honest trust in Christ to casually opt out and take a rain check on obedience to Christ.

In all us believers, reflexes of the old life remain. In Jesus' original disciples, don't we see stubborn, residual prejudices and blind spots that were slow to give way to the light of Christ? So, in all of us, the desires of the Spirit are opposed by a constant undertow and static interference from the flesh (Galatians 5:17). Yes, in combat our courage can blink. Our flesh occasionally may get the best of us. Our faith can falter in the trenches.

Yet, an honest-to-God believer, possessing a saving faith, wants to follow Jesus even unto death if necessary. Would I die for Christ? Only God knows. Like many of us, I have more coward in me than I would like to admit. What I do know is that everything in me wants to be up for that. Where a vital faith exists, one is ashamed whenever his or her follow-through proves weaker than one's good intentions.

The only question is, What qualifies as saving faith? It is one thing to profess faith; it is another to possess it. The thought of false or counterfeit faith should surprise no one familiar with the New Testament. There we are told, for example, of false brethren (2 Corinthians 11:26), false prophets (Matthew 7:15), and false apostles (2 Corinthians 11:13-14). In John 6:66 some of Jesus' "disciples" got fed up and embarrassed with his hard sayings. So they split. They walked no more with Him.

Remember the parable of the sower (Matthew 13) where Jesus describes rootless and fruitless faith? Both pretenders. James (chapter 2:26) speaks of dead faith. On one occasion, John (2:23-25) tells us Jesus refused to acknowledge the "belief" of some in Jerusalem. Why? He saw right through it. It was shallow, not seminal. In a similar way, the Lord challenged (and unmasked) the unbelief of some Jews who, impressed with his many miracles, had ostensibly believed in Him---until He crossed swords with their prejudices (John 8:31ff). In fact, as mentioned above, Jesus warns that at the judgment (Matthew 7:15-23), the faith of some so-called "Christian workers" will be exposed as a fraud. Despite their boast of performing miracles and casting out demons in His name, their godless works will "out" them for the posturers they really were all along.

All during my life and ministry I have been exposed up close and personal with this doctrine of "cheap grace" (sometimes called "easy believism"). I have painfully witnessed where it leads---and that is certainly not in the direction of Christian excellence and a life worth dying for. Where it generally leads is to Presumption City with all the bad things that go with it.

I had classmates in seminary and even knew one pastor, in particular, who occasionally flaunted their excesses, all to make the point that they were not saved by works, but by God's grace. Occasionally they would spout profanity, even using God's name, and call it "grace language." I remember in my seminary teaching days a student (a female ski instructor) who got incensed at the idea that the moral commands of Christ were anything more than noble suggestions she could follow or ignore at her pleasure. It was all about grace, you know.

Yes, grasping the scope and cost of discipleship takes a maturing process. We believers must crawl before we can walk, and walk before we can run. We grow into our adult Christian clothes. The Christian life or discipleship admits to development. It also admits to the potential for disease, just as in the physical life. Growing up we all fall and stumble around some.

Because we are still in the flesh, beset by all its weakness and appetites, infected with cultural influences, and constantly leveraged by the Tempter, we do not always see things as we ought. We do not always make the right choices. We do not always think in a godly fashion. We do not always walk in a straight line behind the Lord. Sometimes, like children who need more discipline, we balk at where He is leading us. His rod and His staff may comfort us, but our flesh will always oppose us.

Spiritual development, we know, is not a straight line upward. Like a graph, it is a lot of jagged lines; some spike sharply upward, some downward, some level spots, but the pattern from the starting point toward the goal trends upward. If we truly trust in Christ for all that He is (again, we do not trust Him selectively or piecemeal), then our instinct is naturally and logically to follow Him where He leads.

If it isn't, something is amiss.

Call it Christianity Lite. Call it Wal-Mart Christianity. McChristianity. Costless, bloodless Christianity. So disgustingly American. A Have-A-Free-Pass-to-Heaven-and-A-Painless-Trip-in-the-World version of Christianity. Call it bogus Christianity. Or, call it "another Gospel" (Galatians 1:6-9), because that is what the Lord is going to call it on the Last Day.

If, however, we really are Christians, truly regenerated and authentic children of God, the Spirit of God grows and matures us so that incrementally we take on real Christian character, walk in the light and pay the price of being different. It's His whole project of conforming His people to the moral image of Jesus Christ. That is not God's wish; it's God's purpose (Romans 8:29).

If what we call "faith" does not materialize in growing conformity in following Christ (or discipleship), then it's just a religious game of "let's pretend." Jesus and the apostles made it so abundantly clear that *real believers are real followers,* that it baffles me that there could be any question about this.

To say to Christ, "I will take You as my Savior, but I refuse to follow You there or to serve You here," or to say to Him, "I will gratefully accept the life You laid down for me, but don't expect me to give mine back in return or be ruled by You," well, that's appalling on the face of it. Such people are like Simon Magnus, "still in the bonds of iniquity" (Acts 8:23). Yet, to all intents and purposes, that is the perverted version of the "Gospel" that has passed and still is passing for evangelical in many churches to this hour. It is a scandal. It cheapens grace beyond words.

As the late Charlie Finley, erstwhile owner of the Oakland Athletics baseball team, once responded dismissively when asked by reporters whether or not a rumored buyer of his club would come through,

"Big hat, no cattle."

A lot of Christian profession is that way: big hat, no cattle. Christian faith comes with walking shoes, not just talking heads. As Bishop J. C. Ryle has said, "everyone God justifies, He also sanctifies" (in the sense of bringing about practical holiness in them). See Hebrews 12:14.

A "faith" that fails to follow is as hollow as a con artist's promises. That "faith" does not yield a life worth dying for. In fact it does not yield a life at all, only a lie that lulls church-goers into a fatal sleep. That is why I call this form of doctrine a serial killer in our churches.

With that kind of theology grooving our brains, it is less likely that one will find the incentive in Christ to go for the gold or go down for the count because it is not all that morally compelling to make our calling and election sure (2 Peter 1:10). And, there is also the perverse notion among the more antinomian types that God's grace is somehow even magnified by the great gap between His pardoning grace and our sinning habits!

If we aspire to a life worth dying for, we must trash any residual of that kind of cheap grace in our thinking and resolve, for the love of Christ, to get fully invested in the race for Christian excellence in all of its radical meaning. Anything less is a caricature of the Christian life.

Let us aspire to be disciples, not religious dilettantes . . . to be contenders, not pretenders. In the game, not playing a game. Not talkers, but walkers. Let us live up to our pedigree in Christ, not down to our family tree in Adam. By grace, let us go for the gold and strive by God's grace to achieve the most difficult and spectacular goal on earth: just excelling at being a Christian.

Chapter 5

Going For the Gold

"Whoever finds his life will lose it, and whoever loses his life for my sake shall find it" (Matthew 10:39).

When my youngest brother, Alan, was getting into his early years in high school, one of our uncles hired him to work on the old family farm to trim Christmas trees and to do other odd jobs. Harold, not a believer, but a very substantial man of considerable character and one equally adept at spotting character in others, had his eye on Alan as an ideal young man he could train for his business enterprises and, eventually, he probably thought, turn things over to him. He told Alan that he could have a great future with him.

> "You come with me, Alan, and you will never need anything."

He really meant that and would have been as good as his word. For any person, especially a high school kid, that had to be a very tempting prospect. Harold was no talker. He knew his business.

The only problem was something his uncle could never understand, Alan was as serious as a stroke about serving Christ, not Mammon. Respectfully, Alan explained to him that, as much as he appreciated his offer and was flattered by his confidence in him, he had other plans and they involved not man's business, but God's.

Uncle Harold was tight with our family, but unlike our little clan he was not in any way, shape or form a religious man. He knew our parents were devout to the core, lived what they believed, and that Alan seemed to be on that same track. But to him, with no eternal perspective, it seemed a crying shame to get so invested in "serving God" when a great world of opportunity beckoned, and he could make it happen for Alan. When Alan seemed to him a little stubborn in his direction, in a bit of exasperation, Harold exclaimed (rough quote):

> "Alan, you can have your religion and all that, but you don't have to be a missionary about it!"

Translation:

> "Look, Alan, a little dab will do ya! You can serve God or whatever, but not so fanatically that you let the opportunity to succeed and excel in life pass you by."

Understanding fully the translation, Alan just smiled in his way, and responded:

> "Uncle Harold, I thank you, but really, I'd rather be a missionary."

And you know what? He was in a way. Eventually, after graduating from Marshall University, he got hooked up with the Navigators, spent his whole career with that organization, retiring just a few years ago as

U. S. Director. People all over the world have been impacted for Christ by his example and leadership. Despite that missed opportunity way back there, he will tell you he doesn't need anything. God is good.

Alan pursued Christian excellence and a life worth dying for, and he has never regretted it for a minute, despite a lot of suffering along the way. And for him, there is laid up in Heaven a greater reward than all the rich uncles in all the world could ever bestow and then some.

Now let's distill that. Let's see how excellence translates in Christian terms at street level. What are its implications for persons whose identity resides, not in a transient occupation, but in an eternal relation to the Lord of the Universe?

Christian excellence is simply pulling out all the stops to live Christianly in every dimension of our existence. It is putting the Christ of Sunday into shoe leather on Monday. So simple, but, ah, so radical. The "program" starts with a strictly Christian agenda and includes, by definition, godly motives in that pursuit. Hence, Christian excellence circumscribes what things we choose to excel in as much as why we strive for them.

To expand upon it a bit, the pursuit of excellence for believers translates to a determined effort to match, as nearly as possible (through the grace of God), what God intended us to be, to do and to believe. At street level on Monday morning, it comes down to an all-out, radical, take-no-prisoners, leave-it-all-on-the-field mission to be a fully functional (as opposed to a merely formal) disciple.

Or put differently, Christian excellence involves selling out for Christ . . . giving our all for the One who sacrificed His all for us. It is satisfied with nothing less than unconditional surrender to the will and ways of God. A fully invested disciple (as opposed to a perfunctory one) is an "utmost for His highest" kind of follower.

Look, I am not saying anything that hasn't been said before by people better and brighter than I am. The problem is that, sometimes, we are so numb and dumb we just don't get it, and therefore don't get after it.

When I was a kid I loved sports, most especially football and basketball. I had good athletic skills and aspired to excel big-time. But there were a few obstacles in the way, the most important of which are germane for my illustrative purposes. You see, in a lot of ways I never really got it. Let me explain.

As I am writing this passage, it is the opening of the 2012 Olympic Games in London. One common denominator binds all those athletes and sportsmen. In their chosen fields of athletic endeavor, they all "got it." Somewhere, somehow they had, I guess, an epiphany. All of us who love sports desire to excel. But all these people *intended* to. And, one way or another, they figured out that on the way to excellence in their sport or event, nothing less than an all-out assault on the peak of their potential would position them to win a championship or walk off with a medal. They got it. All of them understand what I never did as a kid. If you aim to excel, you have to pull out all the stops, leave all half measures behind, dedicate yourself and discipline your body to the pursuit.

It is no different with the pursuit of Christian excellence. The Lord Jesus did not call us to sit on our couches and make pious noises; He called us to take up our crosses and to follow Him. That calling admits of no lounging around, following Christ part of the time and flirting with the world the rest of the time. Somehow we just need to "get it."

A radicalized disciple is truly alive and available to God. And where there is life, there are vital signs such as deeply revering the holiness of God, being invested in the work of God, being compelled by the love of God and being loyal to the Word of God.

With all that in view, it becomes clearer what the New Testament epistles mean when they summon believers to let their minds dwell on excellence (Philippians 4:8) and to keep their behavior excellent among the Gentiles (1 Peter 2:12). The furthest things from the apostles' mind were the kinds of operational and stylistic excellencies that "the streets" make so much ado about. More in keeping with the apostolic vision of excellence are appeals like these:

> "I urge you therefore, brethren, by the mercies of God, present your bodies a living and a holy sacrifice, acceptable to God, which is your spiritual service of worship. And do not be conformed to this world, but be transformed by the renewing of your mind . . ." (Romans 12:1-2).

> " . . . lay aside the old self . . . and . . . be renewed in the spirit of your mind, and put on the new self, which in the likeness of God has been created in righteousness and holiness of the truth" (Ephesians 4:22-24).

> " . . . prove yourselves to be blameless and innocent, children of God above reproach in the midst of a crooked and perverse generation, among whom you appear as lights in the world,

holding fast the word of life . . ." (Philippians 2:15-16).

" . . . we request and exhort you in the name of the Lord Jesus that, as you received from us instruction as to how you ought to walk and please God . . . that you may excel still more and more" (1 Thessalonians 4:1).

"If then you have been raised up with Christ, keep seeking the things above, where Christ is, seated at the right hand of God. Set your mind on the things above, not on the things that are on earth" (Colossians 3:1).

For a Christian, the spirit of true excellence is embodied in sentiments like these:

"I have counted all things to be loss in view of the surpassing value of knowing Christ Jesus my Lord, for whom I have suffered the loss of all things, and count them but rubbish in order that I may gain Christ, and be found in Him . . . that I may know Him, and the power of His resurrection and the fellowship of His sufferings, being conformed to His death . . ."
(Philippians 3:8-10).

"Therefore we have as our ambition . . . to be pleasing to Him" (2 Corinthians 5:9).

"My food is to do the will of Him who sent Me, and to accomplish His work" (John 4:34).

Or, in an agenda like this:

" . . . I will not offer to the Lord burnt offerings which cost me nothing" (2 Samuel 24:24).

" . . . applying all diligence, in your faith supply moral excellence, and in your moral excellence, knowledge and in your knowledge, self-control, and in your self-control, perseverance, and in your perseverance, godliness; and in your godliness, brotherly kindness, and in your brotherly kindness, Christian love. For if these qualities are yours and increasing, they render you neither useless nor unfruitful in the true knowledge of our Lord Jesus Christ. For he who lacks these qualities is blind or shortsighted, having forgotten his purification from his old sins. Therefore, brethren, be all the more diligent to make certain about His calling and choosing you; for as long as you practice these things, you will never stumble; for in this way the entrance into the eternal kingdom of our Lord and Savior Jesus Christ will be abundantly supplied to you" (2 Peter 1:5-11).

"Therefore . . . let us also lay aside every encumbrance, and the sin which so easily entangles us, and let us run with endurance the race that is set before us, fixing our eyes on Jesus . . ." (Hebrews 12:1-2).

By way of contrast, let me differentiate in various respects this conception of Christian excellence with the worldly variety.

The aspiration of conventional excellence is to be outstanding in the world, whereas the chief concern of Christian excellence is to be unstained by the world. The ambition of those who follow the path of traditional excellence is to impress our peers with ourselves; the mission of those who pursue Christian excellence is to win them for Christ. Traditional excellence, at best, is nothing more than Christians excelling at things they do; the signature of Christian excellence, however, is excelling at what we are.

That is the key. There is no Christian excellence until we excel at being Christian. That means being what we are supposed to be in Christ, doing what we are supposed to do, going where we are supposed to go and believing what we are supposed to believe.

So then, Christian excellence is not measured by how well believers surpass others in functional skills and keep pace with cultural fashions, but by how well they keep pace with the Word, the work, the will and the ways of Jesus Christ.

Lest we seem to set the bar impossibly (and therefore discouragingly) high, we need to take account of an important distinction in our quest.

The Spirit versus the Standard of Christian Excellence

There is both the *objective* standard of Christian excellence (to which none of us will ever measure up in this world) and a *subjective* spirit of Christian excellence. The latter is the handmaid of the former. Take heart. Here is some good news. Though we all fall short of the ideal, by grace, the spirit of Christian excellence is well within our reach.

You see, while the standard of Christian excellence is measured by proximity to the ideal, the spirit of Christian excellence is determined by our tenacity in striving for it. It is simply a relentless, grace empowered, time-tested commitment to the ultimate goal. In other words, to own a spirit of Christian excellence, one buys the ideal and pays the price over time in daily installments.

So, for us then, the spirit of excellence is a biblical vision far more exalted and compelling than exhausting ourselves in imitating the peripheral skills and passing fashions that impress the world. What matters most to us is modeling the heavenly Master, not mastering the earthly models.

As believers we refuse to concede to the world the license to set the target of excellence for us. If I aspire to true greatness, I don't have to play by society's arbitrary rules or be measured by its vain standards. There are cultural ideals and then there are Christian ideals, and the latter are the only ones that eternally matter. There is more than one "game" in town. We can reserve the option to take aim at another target, which is far better---not because it is easier, but because it is higher and holier.

We must remember that this world is not our town. Its values are not necessarily our own imperatives. True, we are in the world; yet we are not really of it. Therefore, in our quest for excellence, we are not limited to its narrow stock of options. We have the license (and the moral power in Christ) to take the higher road. On the one less traveled, the rewards are far sweeter and the ideals vastly different. So then, our vision of excellence is no cheap target, but a pursuit vastly superior to, and more noble and radical than, the traditional vision.

At this point, we should talk about what, I believe, is a common obstacle in getting our heads around the vision of excellence I'm selling. For the fact is, if we are confused about who we are, chances are we will be confused about where we are going or what we are doing.

My college experience illustrates the obstacle nicely. I entered college as a journalism major on a football scholarship. Though the backstory is too long to tell, the head of my department had his eye on me. That was going to change my whole sense of identity and send me in a new direction.

Ever since my freshman year in high school, academic things had been secondary to my preferred identity as an athlete. Fortunately, I had enough smarts that I could make the grades (not necessarily the best) without opening a single book. Embarrassing to recall, to be sure.

Nothing changed at the start of my college career. My sister-in-law (now) still shakes her head as she recalls sitting next to me in a Western Civilization class and finding out I made a better grade than she, even though I never took a single note. Although I never thought of myself at the time as an intellectual dolt, the truth was, I had a lot more ambition to excel in athletics than academics. That was my identity then.

At some point that year, W. L. T. Crocker, my department head and erstwhile college football player, summoned me into his office and had a chat with me that dramatically changed my sense of self. I won't go into all that he said, but simply relate that what he shared with me that day was for me a kind of epiphany.

Identity-wise it was a personal paradigm shift. From that conversation, I came away that day no longer envisioning myself as your regular "jock" type, lounging through classes but laying it on the line in practice. No, I came away from that little tête-à-tête with a new life-shifting sense of identity as a person endowed with intellectual powers that could, with focus and nourishment, evolve into intellectual prowess.

Life for me has never been the same. After two years and a limiting injury, I gave up football, as much as I loved it, and finagled (with Crocker's influential assistance) an academic scholarship, shifting my mental orientation from athletics to academics and student leadership. I finished college with a strong resumé after beginning as an indifferent student and a bench-warming freshman football player.

Likewise, in the pursuit of Christian excellence, we can lose sight of who we really are. There must be no muddlement about this. Fogginess here will take us down a bunny trail, and I contend that this is a problem that can sometimes, albeit subtly, throw us off the scent.

Say I'm with a Christian friend at a restaurant, and an acquaintance of mine, Frank, comes along with a buddy of his own en route to their table. But, seeing me, Frank stops to greet me and meet my guest. In the process, he politely introduces his own guest to our table, a fellow named John Doe. Notice how he introduces his dinner guest:

> "Jim, John is an old friend of mine from Chicago. We go back to college days. You guys will be delighted to know that John is a devout Christian attorney back there."

We exchange a few more pleasantries, and as they move toward their table, my dinner guest asks me more about friendly Frank.

> "Oh, you would really like Frank. Great fellow. He is a well-respected Christian orthopedic surgeon around here. Hope you never need him!"

Think a minute about the way we tend to describe fellow believers to other believers who are unacquainted with them. Don't we typically locate the identity of our fellow believers in their occupations or professions, or even in their avocations? Don't we refer to Joe Blow as a Christian writer, or identify Mary Smith as a Christian physicist, or some other as a Christian engineer, or a Christian businessman, or a Christian congressman, or a Christian athlete or a Christian teacher, etc.? Of course.

So what's the point? Simply that this typical mode of describing Christian people tends to mislocate their essential identity (a Christian) and reduce it to a mere modifying circumstance. We elevate a job or profession, which is peripheral to our identity, to something central. This ordinary way of conceiving of our identity, if we happen to be persons who strive to excel, impels us to put our eggs in the wrong basket.

How so?

You see, if I equate my identity with my profession or vocation, then being a Christian is reduced to a sidebar of my identity. Most likely, therefore, I will focus much of my energy trying to excel at the point of my self-perceived identity.

I really believe that the pursuit of excellence, where it exists in Christian circles, misses the road at times just because we fail to grasp that, first and foremost, we are Christians . . . disciples of Jesus Christ before we are anything else. Unless we excel at the point of our true identity, as disciples, it is pretty much irrelevant, in the eyes of God at least, that we excel in our respective vocations (or avocations).

By analogy, that is like a medical doctor excelling at poker, or an engineer being renowned as a fisherman or an architect making waves in motorsports. That is all good as far as it goes; it just doesn't go very far. It doesn't make those people any better in their chosen fields and that is what really matters to those who use their services.

So with us Christians, what ultimately matters is whether we excel at being Christian---the point of our real identity. That is our true vocation. It transcends everything else we might be or do. That is the target above all else that we should aim at and expend ourselves for, even die for.

Let me illustrate how identity confusion misleads one in the pursuit of excellence. Say I am an idealistic Christian educator. In that mode where "educator" dominates my sense of identity, I will naturally set my sights on becoming a great teacher. That is natural, for, as I hold, our ideals are born of our sense of who we are. Yet somehow (it's that awkward "modifying circumstance"!) as a Christian, there is likely to be an underlying sense of something amiss . . . a nagging need to somehow ennoble and sanctify such a sacred expenditure of life on such a mundane goal, i.e., distinguishing oneself as a superlative teacher.

So how do I fix this discomfort with the fact that the "Christian" part of my identity (you know, the modifying circumstance) is not getting as much face time as the educator in what I do? Oh, simple. I just anoint my resolution (to excel as an educator) with the blessed oil of Christian motive. Ah, yes, I will dedicate my pursuit of teaching excellence to the glory of God. Problem solved, right? Hardly. That's a best-case scenario.

The same approach applies to the pursuit of excellence in the other professions. Excellence will always be defined by the standards of that vocation. Therefore its pursuit necessarily focuses on vocational skills and achievements. We "Christianize" and sanctify the quest for excellence by the application of relevant Christian principles.

Well, my contention is that this approach, though well-intentioned, is mistaken and misses the mark by a mile. You see, our identity is not what we do but who we are. And, with a shift in the focus of our identity comes a corresponding shift in the focus of excellence.

To sum up, let us not underestimate this "occupational hazard" in the process of fixing our sense of identity. I don't think this is much ado about nothing. Let me reiterate that, on the contrary, muddle-mindedness here will inevitably drive our pursuit of excellence down a traditional road rather than a biblical one. Fuzziness about our identity will lead us to expend ourselves in the tangential rather than the essential. Subordinating our Christian identity to a mere modifying circumstance of our occupational identity can never change more than the tone of our pursuit of excellence. It can never change its direction.

Now, I concede that in many cases there may not be in fact any such confusion. It is just a conventional and verbally economical way to present two important components of our identity to people to whom both might be of interest. And besides, what is the alternative? Somehow "doctor Christian" seems woefully awkward and unlyrical.

I understand. But let's not miss the point. My point is that our conventions are sometimes more revealing than we suspect. Form tends to follow function. In this case, what seems innocent at first glance may upon closer examination be a Freudian slip. Guardedly, I say "may be." Whether or not it really is depends on our own inner feelings about who we are.

Again, if we are misty at the point of our identity, the fog will spread to our pursuit of excellence. We just need to make very sure that we are crystal clear about who we are in Christ and that we don't confuse our secular occupation with our core identity---disciples of Christ.

Here, I am reminded of the ringing words of Nehemiah, with which he turned aside the efforts of the enemies of the Jews as they sought to deflect the governor from his God-given task:

> "I am doing a great work and I cannot come down" (Nehemiah 6:3).

Let us get zeroed in on our real identity and refuse to be deflected from our true vocation by the brass rings of lesser things.

People choose to excel in some of the dumbest things! Scarfing down a record load of hotdogs comes to mind as supremely stupid and good for nothing but a fleeting moment of face time on the internet. Who cares? That is an extreme case, but, to my mind, an epitome of the vanities that people pursue in the name of excellence for some ephemeral reward. Chasing after wind! At the end of the day, the prize is not worth the trouble.

If there is one thing more than any I would like to get across in this chapter, it is this: The pursuit of any form of excellence other than the Christian vision is a comedown. Again, we are not talking about lowering the bar so the Christian can find a false sense of living up to the standard. We are talking about the only standard that really matters---the gold standard, not fool's gold. And by the grace of God, let everyone who names the name of Christ endeavor to "go for it."

Chapter 6

The Best Way to Go

"Why settle for the inferior when the superior lies within reach?"

On our vacation a few years ago, we were forced to fly into Miami instead of Tampa as usual. From the Tampa airport, access to I-75 South to Naples (our destination) is rather easy. However, getting out of MIA to I-75 North, at least for an outsider, is more difficult. A wrong turn can really mess a person up, especially in the deep of night, and put one in uncomfortable places to say the least, not to mention the risk of an accident due to distraction if one tries to right the ship. So, the second time we flew into MIA, I was doubly careful to determine the best way to go.

Distinctively ***Christian*** excellence is the best way to go. The Christian vision of excellence is an ideal far more ennobling and humanizing than any other that one might pursue in the name of excellence. Its superiority resides in four attributes, which are the racer's edges:

The Christian Vision is Theocentric

First of all, it emerges from a theistic perspective rather than a narcissistic motive. In short, it represents the logical outcome of our relationship to God in

Christ and His purpose in our lives. In contrast, the kinds of excellence to which the world aspires, though not necessarily wrong in themselves, at bottom, are selfishly motivated, and, viewed from an eternal perspective, are less relevant to anything that ultimately matters.

One who has caught the vision of Christian excellence has no patience with "trivial pursuits" which divert him from his high calling. To those ever-present temptations to dissipate his time, gifts, and energies perfecting frivolous competencies in the quest for self-realization, or self-esteem, or self-advancement, his response is again the answer of Nehemiah (Neh. 6:3).

So, the Christian ideal emerges from our biblical mandate. Its pursuit is for God, in Christ, through the Spirit and by grace. The Christian concept is bathed and bundled in theistic convictions.

From a biblical standpoint, excellence merely for excellence's sake is a goal that has no rational sanction. Unless there is a God who has revealed that target in an objective way, who is to say that excellence (of any kind) is something we should strive for? Moreover, who is competent to decide, in the absence of authoritative norms, what is excellent? In their absence, who can say that the pursuit of any given value is superior to its neglect? As the ancient Preacher observed:

> "As is the fate of the fool, it will also befall me. Why then have I been extremely wise? So I said to myself, 'This too is vanity.' For there is no lasting remembrance of the wise man as with the fool, inasmuch as in coming days all will be forgotten. And how the wise man and the fool alike die" (Ecclesiastes 2:15-16)!

So it is for a person living out his life under the sun without God. The pursuit of traditional excellence is not mandated by Reason. Ultimately it makes no difference, and what makes no difference is an exercise in futility and triviality. How right the Preacher was about life under the sun---a vain, monotonous and tediously repetitious litany of apparent inequities in a world with no divine frame of reference:

> "I again saw under the sun that the race is not to the swift, and the battle is not to the warriors, and neither is bread to the wise, nor wealth to the discerning, nor favor to men of ability; for time and chance overtake them all"
> (Ecclesiastes 9:11).

In traditional terms, one might well argue from observation that Chance and Connections advance men as often as Excellence. At least they play a more prominent role in that respect than usually acknowledged. No matter though, for the person who achieves anything in life at the expense of ignoring God, all of his promotions, commendations, medals, plaques, ribbons and trophies are as meaningless as a hearty burp after dinner. Let him count his medals, mount his trophies, display his ribbons, frame his certificates of achievement, collect his clippings and wallow in his wealth. But he had better hurry, because the meter is running. He is on course for a rendezvous with reality. Death is the Great Eraser, the Ultimate Leveler of all small differences in godless men who excelled in ways that never really mattered.

The true measure of the merit of any pursuit is the worth of its purpose. Why else has the medical profession been so highly esteemed over the generations? The simple reason is that the average secular man values nothing more highly than his own preservation and he sees that physicians are dedicated to that purpose. Likewise, scientists are admired and their work more celebrated than the dedicated endeavors of many others because of the perception that their work enhances our well-being.

Given our biblical assumptions, what life goal could possibly rival the nobility of our Christian vision of excellence? If there is a personal God who is really there, One who, through faith in Christ, can be known in a personal way and served with distinction, what could be more worthy of our devotion and the investment of our being than to please Him, to be transformed into His moral likeness and to be mastered by His love . . . to discharge His purpose, to be harnessed to His Spirit and to be charged with His power?

Such a possibility far transcends a mere obligation! An opportunity like that is the "impossible dream." It is a staggering privilege which dignifies my fallen humanity, relieves my life of the burden of insignificance, crowns my existence with Purpose, invigorates my heart with Hope and elevates my spirit with a pervasive touch of the Eternal.

So then, our Christian vision of excellence is founded on a theistic worldview and our pursuit of it is animated by that perspective. Whatever competes with its agenda, or even fails to contribute to it, is not a form of excellence that a believer can afford to achieve. As King Pyrrhus once remarked after a hard-fought triumph over the Romans in southern Italy, "One more victory like that and we'll be ruined." Any form of traditional excellence achieved at the expense or compromise of the Christian vision is actually a defeat, not a triumph.

The Secular Vision is Narcissistic

By contrast, the secular vision of excellence has no better foundation than humanistic narcissism, however disguised. Who can seriously deny that the popular forms of excellence to which people traditionally aspire are usually coveted as a means of establishing one's superiority? People want to be a cut above the common herd . . . to be known as "winners". . . to have access to the fast track . . . to escape confusion with that faceless glob of anonymous humanity fated to be "losers."

Like so many war heroes whose exploits are sometimes animated more by blind fear than steely courage, the drive to excel in conventional ways is not always what it appears to be. Although he or she postures as a lover of excellence, beneath the surface, an achiever often carries a compulsiveness born, not of superior standards, but of deep seated insecurity, of an overpowering fear of failure and of the need to reassure oneself, or others, that one is not really like all the rest.

That form of self-obsessed pride we call "narcissism" or "selfism" or "me-ism." Because it cloaks itself in the pious pretense of nobler ideals, it manages to evade the contempt reserved for more blatant manifestations of the same malaise of the human spirit.

If that critique seems harsh or unfair, just ask yourself this question: What forms of excellence can you think of that could survive the absence of the promise of applause, or public recognition or financial rewards that set one person apart from another? In almost any field one can imagine---the arts, athletics, business, science, the professions---excellence, to the extent that it exists, has been and must continue to be nurtured by the promise of some kind of recognition that enlarges the ego of the achiever. In contradistinction, the Christian vision is superior because of its inclusiveness.

The Christian Vision is Inclusive

The superiority of the Christian vision of excellence also appears in its *inclusiveness* versus the *exclusiveness* of the secular alternative. We believe in the power of the ordinary to be extraordinary. Previously, we observed that every category of traditional achievement requires for its attainment some natural, inherited or acquired advantage not equally accessible to the masses. Excellence in the normal conception is not a "land of equal opportunity."

There is no intention on my part to minimize or to disparage the accomplishments of people of achievement. Whatever edges one may have enjoyed in his pursuit of a secular form of excellence, the price of distinction was still high, and hard-won skills should be appreciated as monuments of immense effort.

Still, one of the greatest myths in life is the lie with which so many well-intentioned parents indoctrinate their children: "You can be anything you want to be."

For a few people that might be so; for the majority, life is heartlessly inequitable. Nature is obviously no Marxist, for its wealth of assets is not distributed equally, neither to nations nor individuals. Circumstances favor some and immutably exclude others. If anyone doubts this, try to name, if you can, one coveted form of excellence that affords to all-comers exactly the same opportunity. I can't think of a single one!

And, the tarnish on the secular model dulls it even more when you consider that a great many people are so very average in almost every way---mentally, physically, emotionally, socially and financially---that the attainment of excellence, for them, in any popular category is frankly out of the question. If it were only a matter of will or of commitment, then average people would at least have a shot at it, although not an equal one. So, for ordinary people, excellence in its conventional varieties is like a museum artifact something they can admire but not acquire. It is tainted with all the exclusiveness of a country club. These are not ideals that ordinary people can hitch their wagon to.

The refreshing difference in the Christian vision is it is not elitist, but egalitarian. The beauty of it is that ordinary people can be extraordinary. The average man can be exceptional in the ways that really matter. For excellence in the Christian definition does not require that I be the best, or even among the best, in the performance of some skill. What it really demands is that I give my best to become all that God meant me to be and to discharge all that God meant for me to do.

The ideal is to give my best, to be my best and to do my best with respect to the purposes of God for my life. Realistically, no one can every minute of every day achieve that ideal. We are fallen people, still becoming by the grace of God what we ought to be. We are far from finished products. Hence, the badge of Christian excellence on the process side is not so much winning the battle, as battling to win. And, the signs that are most indicative of that spirit of excellence are evidences of intensity and consistency in carrying out our Christian mandate. This form of excellence is equally accessible to any believer. What it takes is relentless commitment. Any default has its roots in disinterest, not disadvantage.

Where this kind of dedication to the process exists, excellence in the form of progress is bound to follow. But progress takes time; excellence in process takes only effort---and that is something anybody can give. It is a way that every believer can excel. Ordinary people can be extraordinary. Average people can be truly exceptional, in a way that really matters in the eyes of the most important Person in the universe.

We must not underestimate the importance this form of excellence is in the sight of God. For example, in the Parable of the Talents (Matthew 25:14ff) the servant who energetically managed the less generous resources (the two talents) entrusted to him by his Master is not praised less lavishly for his excellence than the one who faithfully utilized his more abundant endowments (the five talents). God, in judging His servants, is not so concerned with *quantity* of output as He is with *quality* of input.

Another striking example of this divine criterion is the case of the widow's mite (Mark 12:41ff). Although her gift was exceedingly small, relatively speaking, it was her all. Jesus evaluated her offering, not by what she gave *per se*, but in light of what she had to give.

That standard of measure is the hope of ordinary people who, in *this* world, will never have a chance to take their bows or gain recognition for a job well done. All the honors passed around in this unjust world are reserved for an elect few. Excellence in the conventional sense is the exclusive domain of the superbly gifted.

This quest to excel conventionally requires no special input that God has not already made available. What it does require is extraordinary output. Nothing but your own indolence can deny you access to the "winners" circle. From a biblical perspective, however, there is no true excellence without exertion equal to one's endowments, for the spirit of excellence is as conditioned to exertion as it is to perfection. Great achievements born of idle energy are no more than the illegitimate offspring of irresponsible genius; they have no rightful claim to the distinguished pedigree of Christian excellence.

The Christian Vision is Anchored to Fixed Ideals

The Christian vision of excellence is again superior to its secular counterpart in that its ideals are fixed or absolute, whereas the latter are hopelessly relative. The reason that our ideals are fixed and immutable is that they are rooted in the unchanging moral nature of God and His revealed will for our lives. The knowledge of His character and His will is accessible to us by means of objective revelation in the form of the Scriptures. The fact that some dispute the credibility of our claim in no way refutes the legitimacy of it. Our confidence in the Bible as a source of revelation is anchored by three strong taproots: our experience in the Word, our experience of it and corroborating evidence outside it.

Given that immovable foundation, the Christian has a fail-safe compass for getting his fixes on the issues of life. We may misread it, but it will not mislead us. Not only do we possess a touchstone of right and wrong, but also we have a yardstick for distinguishing what ultimately matters from what merely seems to.

Because we possess in the Scriptures a "pipeline" to the knowledge of God and the behavior that is, and is not, appropriate for His creatures, we can with their guidance make indisputable value judgments about the issues they address. Only one who takes this ground can logically pontificate about values and ideals.

If God has not spoken, one cannot know, as Francis Schaeffer once stressed, whether it is better to help a little old lady across the street or push her down in front of a car. In the absence of a revelation from God, on what authority can anyone be certain that one act is morally superior to the other?

In rejecting the supernatural realm and the claims of Scripture, the secularist has left himself hopelessly adrift on the waves of relativity. Rationally, he has lost his license to talk about truth in any fixed sense and to make any value judgments based upon it. Everything is in flux. Ideals that were in vogue yesterday are passé today. And who can say with any authority which is better? His problem is deeper than it might seem. It is not simply that he does not know what the truth is; rather, that he is now in no position to know if truth even exists.

However, the believer can say, "I know . . . ," not because he is intellectually arrogant, but because he believes God has spoken in an objective way, i.e., in a propositional and therefore examinable form. By contrast the most the unbeliever can say logically is, "I think . . . ," because he has no sure starting point.

No wonder then we say the Christian vision of excellence is superior. It is a vision that rests on better authority. It rests on pilings of absolutes that do not give way to the shifting tides of philosophical opinion or bend before the winds of fickle fads and temporal fashion.

Now, just because our vision of excellence is shaped by the absolutes of revelation, one should not infer that we believe everything is black or white, or that nothing is relative. That certainly is not the case.

For example, my Christian vision of excellence demands holiness. The unchanging validity of that ideal derives from the eternal purity of the moral nature of God and is substantiated by revelation. However, the expression of that separateness may vary in some respects from generation to generation and from culture to culture.

In the early Greco-Roman culture, a Christian woman wearing short-cropped hair may have sent the wrong message. If, in that day, such a "coiffure" signaled a promiscuous woman, today it says nothing of the sort. In view of that cultural difference, a Christian woman today may take a liberty that one could ill afford in the first century. The principle of separation never changes; the practice of it may.

On the other hand, adultery is explicitly and absolutely condemned in Scripture. In such a case, the believer would insist that nothing can ever become right which is at variance with what is right absolutely. In other words, nothing can *become* true which contradicts what *is* true.

It would also be false to infer that, because the Christian uses revelation as his polestar to get his intellectual fixes on reality and morality, he rejects reason. To subordinate reason to revelation is not the same as renouncing reason in favor of revelation. The believer recognizes that reason is in one respect like money: a great servant, but a bad master.

The believer uses revelation much like an explorer uses a compass. The compass determines the right course and reason follows it. Reason is of great value in reading a compass, but it is a poor substitute for one. To use railroad imagery, the train of Christian reason runs long and hard on the tracks of revelation. Revelation simply keeps reason under control and on course.

Secular conceptions of excellence entail value judgments, which imply standards or ideals. The trouble is that more often than not these standards are arbitrary and subject to change with time. They are not anchored to anything better than tradition, or perhaps, standards arbitrarily prescribed by those in authority at the moment. There are few if any areas of secular endeavor in which the standards of excellence remain unchanged over long periods. All judgments are afflicted with instability.

In this matter of excellence the people of God have the racer's edge by far. By now, I feel sure that the superiority of the distinctly Christian vision of excellence vis-à-vis the more traditional kind is abundantly clear. Having proved this point, now I ask the question, "Is there *any* place for Christians to pursue excellence in these areas?"

The answer is a resounding, Yes, but with qualifications. To that subject we now turn.

Chapter 7

Any Place for Traditional Excellence?

"Christians should elevate the ideals of Heaven, subordinate the ideals of humanity and repudiate the twisted values of a sinful world."

Unlike many men, I grew up rather unskilled (except in athletics). Though my dad certainly taught me to work hard, he never taught me (and I did not take the trouble to learn) to fix cars, frame a house, make furniture, paint pictures, play a musical instrument or any one of a number of other enhancing skills that would have made me more useful (especially to my wife) and certainly a lot less boring to everybody else.

In one way, I have always regretted that because I would love to have acquired any of those skills, or all of the above, especially building things. Man, how I would have liked to have owned a well-equipped shop and built beautiful furniture, or to be able to remodel a house like so many men I know, or to play a violin.

However, I have mentioned to my wife several times over the years, as much as I regret being so unhandy or unskilled in those ways, in another way I am glad. For, had I acquired some of those competencies in my youth, as worthwhile and admirable as they are, possession of them would have diverted me from my narrow focus on the ministries which God gave me. Some men (or women), wired up differently, can and do manage these tensions well, but I doubt that I would have. What I did, however, was make sure that in this life, in which there is such a rivalry for my time and skills, the main thing stayed the main thing. That was my moral imperative. Let's talk about that whole issue.

A Tension arising from Dual Citizenship

Though we are in the world, we Christians are not really of it. Yet we *are* members of the human family. There is a tension between *Whose* we are and *where* we are. Somehow we must **adapt** to the world without **adopting** it. As those having a sort of dual citizenship, we are confronted with three sets of values or ideals.

Kingdom Values

The first and most important ideals are those of the New Order, i.e., those that become us as a New Race in Christ and represent the values of an eternal perspective. Subsuming all others are the ideals of love and holiness. Of course, these values are not two different ideals, but are really flip sides of each other: love expressing our proper relation to God and our neighbor, and holiness expressing our proper relation to all that God declares to be evil, namely, the duty of separation from it.

Human Values

Secondly, there are those values or ideals that we share in common with all humans *as humans*. Such would include beauty, order, functionality, unity in diversity, precision, speed, strength, endurance and so forth.

Worldly Values

Thirdly, there are those values and ideals that reflect the dominion of Satan over a world of fallen men. These might include such pursuits as wealth, power, fame, superiority, revolution or pleasure.

Resolution of the Tensions

Christians should elevate the ideals of Heaven, subordinate the ideals of humanity and repudiate the ideals of a sinful world. Our vision of Christian excellence starts then with the pursuit of all that God has called us to be and all that He has called us to do. Our thirst for excellence may extend beyond the spiritual spectrum of ideals. However, the quest for other forms of excellence must never be allowed to rival this pursuit or to compromise it, but only to complement it.

The Risk of Inversion of Priorities

Even here, as mentioned earlier, there is the risk, however inadvertent, of the misappropriation of honor. Also, there is a danger of shooting ourselves in the foot with good intentions. As the saying goes, "When we are up to our armpits in alligators, it is hard to remember that we came to drain the swamp." We can become so preoccupied with polishing some skill that our souls go to rust. It can be useful for believers to excel in traditional ways, but never at the expense of our spiritual ideals or mission. I am not saying the two are necessarily incompatible; rather, the two are not the same. Moreover, the former (i.e., the traditional) is secondary to the latter (i.e., the spiritual). If the secondary becomes primary, it becomes more of a detriment than a complement to our mission. This topic needs some amplification.

Recognizing the frenetic pace of modern life and the obvious limits of our time and energies, we must consider the propriety of selective default to mediocrity. Is it really important that a Christian strive to excel in everything that he or she undertakes? Our brief response is that, as in matters of social responsibility, our obligation to excellence is hierarchical.

This bottom line is this: The pursuit of Christian excellence is so all-absorbing that no believer can afford the luxury of pursuing any forms of traditional excellence except those that are compatible with and complementary to his spiritual goals. Even those that are perceived to be compatible with and complementary to his commitment to spiritual excellence, the believer must evaluate and give right-of-way to those pursuits that are most contributory to the discharge of his mandate as an ambassador of the Kingdom of God in an alien society. To misappropriate our time, our energies and our resources in the pursuit of some spiritually unfruitful, but ego-flattering form of excellence, is the spiritual equivalent of embezzlement.

Excellence, in general, profits from a "steady gaze" and spiritual excellence more than any. Distraction is a termite that weakens the timber of our commitment. So, we must be careful not to allow our focus to get too diffused across an incoherent spectrum of interests and avocations. So, we have to **prioritize** the distribution of our energy-capital according to our special purpose on this planet.

Priorities pivot on Purpose.

Let me illustrate by an industrial analogy how true this is. It will help us to see: 1) how the Christian must sort out his priorities, and also 2) how sometimes the world and the Christian can have a shared interest in a traditional form of excellence, but not from a common motive.

Take, for example, the disparate purposes for which the chairman of General Motors and the president of the United Auto Workers exist respectively.

The mandate of the GM chief is to make GM attractively profitable for its stockholders to whom he is accountable. They simply want a fair return on their investment. The UAW boss, on the other hand, is accountable, not to the stockholders, but to his union members who want a fair wage, good benefits, job security and good working conditions. In short, his mandate is to maintain provident jobs for his union members.

Because their purposes differ, the priorities of these two leaders will predictably vary. For example, the GM chairman, with his eye on appropriate profits, will naturally move to the top of his list those endeavors that will enhance profitability. Heading the list will be such concerns as operational efficiency and employee productivity. As a direct result of such priorities, the company executive may move to close outdated plants, demand in contract negotiations union "givebacks" and bargain for work rule changes which would allow management more flexibility in the use of labor.

The UAW executive will likely oppose this agenda because he is accountable to someone else who has delivered to him a different mandate that dictates, in this case, a set of priorities not wholly compatible with the former. Whereas the GM head is preoccupied with getting more work for less money, the union chief is trying to figure out how to get more money for less work. The former wants to close plants, curtail benefits and reduce the work force; the latter fights to keep factories open, upgrade or maintain benefits and preserve jobs.

Sometimes, despite the different purposes for which the two executives exist, their interests do intersect, although not for the same motives and not necessarily at the same level of concern. For instance, observe in this analogy that both interests have a stake in the profitability of GM. If the corporation fails (close call in 2008!), the union members are unemployed. However, while the UAW president shares that concern with his company counterpart, the profitability of GM is not his main concern nor does he care about the same level of profit as the corporate boss. In any case, both do have a mutual interest in the profitability of the corporation.

Another example of this shared interest might be in the area of foreign auto imports. The company, for example, may lobby in Congress for an import quota on the grounds that certain automakers enjoy a competitive advantage over U. S. manufacturers. The union may join this effort to influence congressional legislation, not because it cares a flip for GM stockholders, but because any weakening of the GM sales position threatens the jobs of union members.

I believe this analogy serves well to illustrate the way our perceived purpose impacts our priorities. The target determines the way I aim the gun. A sense of his purpose on this planet enables a Christian to sort out more intelligently what matters much, what matter less and what doesn't make a dime's worth of difference.

Priorities are just a list of chores that Purpose gives us, telling us how we should serve her and in what order. Or, to put it another way, Priority is just the path Purpose takes en route to Fulfillment. So then, our Christian commitment to spiritual excellence does not necessarily preclude the right or deny the need to excel sometimes in traditional ways. There is nothing inherently wrong with Christian achievement in conventional categories.

The tests of legitimacy are compatibility and complementarity. But even there, sifting is required.

Not everything compatible with my Christian profession is equally beneficial to my Christian mission. So, I must consider my limits and rank my priorities with a view to confining my focus to those excellencies which are most efficient in discharging the purpose for which Christ bought me with His blood.

Therefore, a Christian is obliged to renounce any secular form of excellence that is incompatible with his or her biblical mandate to adorn the doctrine of God (Titus 2:10) and inconsistent with the calling of the Church as "a chosen race, a royal priesthood, a holy nation, a people for God's own possession, that you may proclaim the excellencies of Him who has called you out of darkness into His marvelous light . . ." (1 Peter 2:9).

Types of Traditional Excellence

Consider the categories into which traditional forms of excellence fall from a Christian perspective. Some are plainly inconsistent, others are simply insignificant and all are secondary to Christian priorities.

Some Incompatible with Christian Profession

Take the first kind. Some people excel in ways that are off limits to a believer. No doubt, to some people, belly dancing is an "off Broadway" art form. Among the connoisseurs and practitioners of this "art" there are ideals or standards that set the amateurs apart from the pros. Some have mastered the techniques; others clearly have not. The former excel in that class of activity; the latter do not approximate the ideal among those who value that skill.

Now, for a believer, this form of excellence is inappropriate. It is lewd and sensual and bent on sexual arousal. Under no conditions could such activity glorify God or edify man. A product of the flesh, it appeals to the flesh alone. As such, it is *verboten* for a Christian, since it is incompatible with our purpose. Likewise, there are prostitutes, con men, counterfeiters, burglars and pickpockets who excel in their vices. These are extraordinarily good at what they do, measured by the standards of those who practice and "police" such activities. But these forms of excellence, obviously, are not options for a believer. These types of traditional excellence are perverse in form. Therefore, they are inappropriate for Christians absolutely.

However some traditional forms of excellence can become inappropriate functionally. That is, the pursuit may be legitimate, but the purpose or motive of it is debased and unworthy from a biblical perspective.

Any goal pursued out of narcissistic or humanistic motives is incompatible with a Christian standard of excellence. The former aspires to glorify self and the latter to glorify man. The Christian, of course, is obliged in whatever he does, to glorify God (1 Corinthians 10:31) in everything and to "adorn the doctrine of God" (Titus 2:10).

On the other hand, just because we are "in the world but not of it" does not, as discussed earlier, entail proscribing *all* popular values, or common interests, or areas of shared commitment with the secular society surrounding us. Even though the grace of God has reoriented our spiritual center in the Kingdom of Heaven, our calling obliges us to renounce only those values that arise from our fallenness, not those rooted in our humanness.

This distinction between ideals anchored in my **generic humanity** and in my **fallen humanity** is significant. The former I may share with other men; the latter I must reject as ideals for any man.

For example, it is my generic humanity, not my fallen humanity, which admires such things as beauty, order, rhythm, logic, strength, speed and agility. Because we are human beings originally created in the image of God, some such values are simply echoes of His imprint upon us, being among those attributes that set us apart from mere brutes. Such affinities reflect the residue of His likeness in us, however distorted by the Fall.

Once, however, our primeval innocence perished in the Fall, our moral depravity has managed to defile ideals *legitimate in themselves* by setting them above the God who is the author and source of every form of excellence. Because I am also a fallen human being, there is the tendency **not simply to admire these attributes, but to idolize them or to corrupt them.** A fallen man might make a fetish of beauty, and thus, art becomes a god, plunging its worshipper into idolatry. So also with power; its lover becomes a tyrant or a sycophant.

However, our well-documented ability to pervert what is good in itself for evil uses is no reason to deny the validity of human values that stem from our humanness and not from our fallenness.

Some Simply Frivolous

Finally, some forms of secular excellence are not incompatible with our profession; they are simply **insignificant** in terms of our purpose. That is because they contribute little or nothing to the discharge of our Christian mandate. Typically these are the excellencies of the bored, the idle and the superficial, and they represent achievement gained at great expense with little return.

So many activities (potentially at least) fit into this category, especially youthful fads. Considered from the vantage point of our purpose, of what value to our Christian mission is skill in video games and hacky sack?

I am not saying such peripheral skills (such as sports) cannot be turned to advantage in our mission. Of course they can. But one must ask the question: Is the investment of time and energy in perfecting such frivolous skills out of proportion to the dividends, in terms of my purpose for being?

I speak as a former scholarship athlete. Even at my "geriatric" stage, until recently, I still liked to mix it up with students playing touch football and basketball. And in the past, I have been more skilled than average at such pastimes as ping-pong, billiards and roller-skating. My desire is not to **condemn** such sidelines and hobbies, but to **caution** us.

I personally have found these avocations rapport-builders in certain contexts. They give me a natural access to people to whom otherwise I might have difficulty finding a bridge. And everybody, including Christians, needs some recreational outlets and mental and emotional diversions. Sure, it's OK to play tennis or golf. However, if on the links I am shooting in the low 80's, it is possible that such skill represents an over-commitment to a peripheral form of excellence. There is a point of diminishing returns when the time and energy I am investing in an activity far exceeds any realistic expectation of a proportional return for my mission in life. Its input into my purpose is negatively disproportionate to the output that excellence requires in that area.

Let's face it. Some proficiencies are, relatively speaking, a waste of time and energy. A Christian has a higher agenda. Let us be occupied with matters that count for time and eternity.

I am appalled at the tendency of Christian parents and kids to overcommit to "junk food" activities. Call it the **tyranny of the trivial,** the great subverter of true excellence. Little League, dance lessons, scouts, clubs, you name it . . . we push our kids harder in these trivial things than in spiritual endeavors. It is not the involvements that I condemn; it is the imbalance with a tilt toward the trivial, at the expense of divine imperatives. Perhaps a family illustration will serve our point.

Early on, my younger daughter developed an almost obsessive interest in gymnastics, a wholesome activity. Nothing about it was incompatible with our Christian worldview. However, we discouraged it (we did not forbid it) because that interest was too peripheral to her career goal of piano performance.

As worthwhile as gymnastics may have been in itself, we explained to her that in terms of her musical ambitions, gymnastics would probably be counterproductive. To achieve the level of skill she aspired to musically would take years of single-minded concentration. If she tried to split her time between the two, chances are she would not excel in either. Anything that gymnastics might contribute to her piano performance would be marginal in comparison with what an equal time investment in piano practice would contribute to her development.

Besides, the benefits of gymnastics would endure only briefly. Even if she became an Olympian, she would be washed up before she hit 20. On the other hand, we pointed out, her piano skills could be enjoyed by herself and others for a lifetime. As a Christian, her musical abilities could be employed in the praise of God and in enhancing the worship of others. Our argument made sense to her. While she continued to follow gymnastics and to dabble around in it on her own, she never pursued it competitively.

I think we need to choose our excellencies more rationally. If we would evaluate our pursuits and proficiencies in terms of their worth to our cause, some of our proud abilities that we have so squanderously cultivated look pretty silly against the backdrop of eternity.

We need to major in our divine mandate, not in cultural minors.

Plutarch, the pagan Greek historian, wrote:

> The emperor Augustus once caught sight of some wealthy foreigners in Rome, who were carrying about young monkeys and puppies in their arms and caressing them with a great show of affection. We are told that he then asked whether the women in those countries did not bear children, thus rebuking in truly imperial fashion those who squander upon animals that capacity for love and affection which in the natural order of things should be reserved for our fellow man. In the same way, since nature has endowed us with a lively curiosity and love of knowledge, we ought equally to blame the people who abuse these gifts and divert them to objects which are unworthy of attention, *when they neglect those which have the best claim to it."* (The emphasis is mine; from *The Rise and Fall of Athens*, Penguin Classics, p. 165.)

That same logic was in the mind of one Antisthenes who, having been told that Ismenius was an excellent oboe player, retorted:

> "Then he must be good for nothing else, otherwise he would never play the oboe so well!"
> (p. 166)

A little later Plutarch comments (p. 166):

> " . . . a man who occupies himself with servile tasks proves by the very pains which he devotes to them that he is indifferent to higher things."

Ancient pagans obviously were not uncritical admirers of just any form of excellence. There were "higher things" and less consequential things. Christians, above all, should acknowledge that distinction and give right of way to it.

Trendy skills may draw the praise of men, but not the praise of God. True excellence would be better served if we pleased God rather than played to the secular gallery. Let others master the surfboard; let us master the Scriptures. Too long we Christians have been excellent at play and remained incompetent to pray. Let us stick to our knitting. What are the things that matter . . . really?

Why should a believer know golf better than he knows God? And, shame on us when we train our animals better than we train our children, when we keep our houses cleaner than our minds, and when we know how to manage money better than our mouths. Shame on us when we push Amway harder than the Way and when we can find our way in the woods better than our way in the Word.

How long will we suffer this tyranny of the trivial and be mastered by the meaningless? How long will we run better than we walk?

As I've said, some things are wrong in themselves; others are foolish in comparison. Sometime we need to clear the nonsense from our agendas. If we are to pursue Christian excellence and a life worth dying for, the Imperial Imperatives require our undivided attention.

I, for one, have little patience for any preaching or teaching that is absent its "Monday morning" significance. What does Christian excellence look like on Monday morning? Theory and concepts are fine, but at the end of the day, I want to know how it all translates to the streets.

So, now let us turn to close encounters with a better kind, people I have known well who are as serious as a heart attack about following Jesus. None of them are perfected people by any stretch, but all of them are surrendered folk who embody that aspiration to live up to their pedigree and to shine in the surrounding darkness for Christ.

Chapter 8

Close Encounters with a Better Kind

"The majesty of kings is no rival to the glory of Christ reflected in ordinary men."

When my younger daughter, Juli, was 10, she was nearly killed in a horseback riding accident (a story recounted in my book, *Polishing God's Monuments: Pillars of Hope for Punishing Times*). We were on a family outing at Oglebay Park in Wheeling, West Virginia, during our annual vacation back East to see our folks. For the better part of the next month, Juli was laid up in the Ohio Valley Hospital, where we became temporary fixtures.

In the bed beside Juli's, during the last two weeks of her stay, was a little girl, slightly younger, named Karen. Karen was the victim of one of the worst cases of parental physical abuse I personally have ever encountered. Those savages mauled her so badly that half the skin had been torn loose from her little skull. Not just once, but on two occasions!

Now she just laid there, vegetating, rolling two of the most beautiful eyes nature could form and making pitiful, unintelligible sounds. Every day, a little Pentecostal woman would come in, as regularly as the sun rises, to spend hours at her bedside and to roll her bed up and down the halls of the children's section. When Mrs. Morris couldn't make it for some reason, one of her daughters, one of whom was a nurse, would come and tend the little thing just as faithfully.

At first, I thought Mrs. Morris must be a relative. Then she told me that she had adopted Karen. This little girl had absolutely nothing to give back that any of us could see (other than what gleamed for Mrs. Morris from those precious eyes). This relationship involved nothing but giving and enormous hardship and sacrifice. Yet, Mrs. Morris gave herself so lovingly to that child! In fact, I learned that she had, earlier in life, adopted even the daughters who now helped her so faithfully, all from difficult circumstances.

Mrs. Morris was the very embodiment of excellence in discipleship. This is the greatness of Christian spirit that crowns ordinary people with majesty of character that no aristocratic pedigree can bestow. By God's grace, the extraordinary is well within the spiritual reach of ordinary people. "Little" Christian people like these, whom we all know, prove it every day. As a prism refracts a beam of sunlight, so also in the lives of great Christians, the majestic hues of Christ-like excellence are refracted by the Spirit of God for all who have eyes to see.

The crown-bearers of Christian excellence, I find, often reflect its presence in some outsized grace, one that distinguishes them from the ordinary in some way as peculiarly Christlike. It is as though the grace of God, although irradiating the whole redeemed character in a measured way, focuses itself with laser-like intensity in specific "muscles" of one's spiritual anatomy. In other words, the spirit of excellence often breaks through in heroic flashes of particular Christian virtues. In one case it may be a refracted glimpse of His unconditional love; in another, a dramatic reflection of

His amazing self-sacrifice, or His unstinting forgiveness that surpasses understanding or His unflinching endurance for the glory of God the Father. In others, this spirit of Christian excellence manifests itself in heroic faith, or uncompromising obedience, or stupendous generosity, or prophetic courage, or magnificent self-control or in some other such prodigy of godliness. Whatever face it may wear, in those who transcend the ordinary, some virtue of Christ is usually highly accentuated. Like a ring bedecked with diamonds, the setting is so artfully designed that one jewel stands out above (but not apart from) its companions.

Perhaps it sounds as though I am confusing spiritual gifts with spiritual character. If so, it is only because a few spiritual gifts (e.g., serving, giving and faith) are in fact moral or spiritual attributes super-added or gloriously intensified by the Holy Spirit. These, we should mention, are most prominent in our *ways* when the Holy Spirit is most dominant in our *wills.*

To illustrate all this, let me draw upon a few examples from my own narrow circle of acquaintances, not because these folk are the most stellar models, but simply because I know them well and bear witness that they are genuine to the core. With some pride, I will begin with some in my own family circle.

There may never be a context more fitting than this for to me to pay belated tribute to my godly parents, in whom I first saw a spirit of authentic discipleship exemplified. Many of you doubtless could second the motion for your own parental models. Mine came to play.

My parents, now deceased, would have blushed at my eulogy. My dad would have waved it off and quickly pointed to all the cracks in his walls (though he did quite mistakenly believe my mom was near perfect). Not every corner was perfectly squared in either of them. Here, however, we are talking about the spirit of Christian excellence, not its unblemished attainment. Even so, for my money, their fidelity to their Christian calling always seemed to me more obvious than any chinks I ever detected in their armor.

For example, how many people reared in a Christian home could sincerely say that they never remember seeing or hearing a single thing in their home life that was morally or ethically inconsistent with their parents' Christian profession? I honestly can, if you can believe it. I am proud to be the grateful beneficiary of a spiritual heritage *that* consistent. They lived daily what they believed.

Whatever domestic errors my parents committed were mostly blunders of the head, not blatant sins of the heart. Their judgment could at times have been impeached, but, at least in my eyes, never their integrity. My parents themselves would disown that assessment as a romantic memory of the reality, but I stand by it. And, coming from the son who gave them the most headaches (by far) growing up, my testimony should be even more credible. What a legacy to leave a child!

So many memories of the priorities of our home are on display in my mental archives, but one vignette is special. We were living in Pratt, West Virginia. It was Christmas morning and I was 7 or 8 years old. The family had just finished opening gifts, when, as an afterthought, I ventured one last long look under the tree to make sure I hadn't missed any goodies.

Good thing, for there, partially hidden in the tree skirt toward the back, was something that lit my boyish eyes . . . a shiny, silver Boy Scout knife with all those neat gadgets! I was prouder of that knife than a little girl with a new doll.

After breakfast that morning, I manfully stuffed my new knife in my little pocket and headed out to play with my friends. It was one of those rare Christmas days when unseasonably warm weather allowed all the kids to turn out and parade their new toys. Pratt, a small town of 900 or so, was just one big playground for kids. That day we canvassed it from east to west and pole to pole. But what I remember most vividly is returning home later that afternoon and discovering my handsome knife missing from my pocket.

My heart sank in my socks. Big tears bolted from my eyes as I began to cry. I had lost my knife! There was no way I would ever find it, because we had covered too much ground that day. It could have happened anywhere. Finding it would be like hunting for the proverbial needle in a haystack. It was a lost cause. I was heartbroken. Seeing my tears, my dad asked me,

"What's the matter, Jimmy?"
"I lost my knife," I blubbered.

Now, had he been an ordinary father, he would have tried to console me by reassuring me that we could find it, and if not, that he would get me another. Instead, whether by premeditation or spiritual instinct, Dad seized the moment and exploited the opening as a window for introducing a little boy to the care and power of God.

"Jimmy," he suggested, "let's go in the bedroom and pray about it. We'll ask the Lord and maybe He will help us find your knife."

There in my parents' bedroom, Dad got down on his knees beside me and we both prayed. My father knew a lost knife was no crisis in Heaven. God is not running a lost and found department for little boys' toys. Still, Dad was wise enough to know, in the words of Leland Ryken, that in God's dealings with us "a thoroughly mundane event [can become] invested with a sense of ultimate spiritual destiny." So, Dad invited God to help me find my knife.

What an audacious faith! To put God on the spot like that . . . and in front of a youngster at such an impressionable age . . . and especially such a volatile, high-spirited one, as my parents well knew, with more than the average potential for going bad.

Rising from his bedside after praying, Dad then took the gutsiest step of all. "Now let's go look for that knife," he offered, pulling out all the stops and going for broke. "Let ***us*** . . ."---I still marvel at a man like that with his faith in his boots.

The next five minutes are branded in my memory forever. In retrospect, those minutes were some of the most formative in my life.

Out the front door we went, across the porch, down a couple of steps, out a short walk and past the front hedge. Then, as if to retrace my tracks, we turned up the street toward my friend Bingy's house, about three doors up the block, looking intently as we walked. At Bingy's place we decided, at random, to cross to the other side of the street. We stepped off the sidewalk . . . across the grass divider . . . crossed the pavement

. . . onto another grass island. Why, there it was! Shining up at me like a diamond in the rough. Embedded in the grass, right in plain view, unmolested, yet so available to any alert passerby! We hadn't been out of the house even five minutes!

That incident is staked out in my mind as my first brush with the reality of God. My father took seriously his parental mandate to rear his children "in the training and instruction of the Lord" (Ephesians 6:3 NIV). With a clear eye for the future, my parents did their part to "buy" me stock in the Rock. How different from so many other parents who pour themselves into their kids, "positioning them for success" in a world going bankrupt and admiring their progress as they compete for the opportunity to slop the Devil's hogs.

The spirit of Christian excellence so evident in my father inhabited my mother also. So often in a marriage where you have one exceptional person, closer inspection will reveal two. Eagles flock to eagles even if they don't always look like birds of a feather. As with my dad, nothing about my mother's "resumé" would stop a hiccup. Yet behind that ordinary façade was a Christian woman of rare mettle. There was never the slightest doubt about the seriousness of her intent to follow Christ.

Nothing epitomizes her attitude more than her indomitable faith and reverence in the face of almost chronic adversity. Many have suffered much more; few have endured affliction much better. If physicians were prophets, Mom would have gone the way of all flesh at 45, though she actually lived to 72. Almost as far back as I can remember, my mother was up and down health-wise, rebounding from serial surgeries, suffering deathly flare-ups from chronic pancreatitis and fighting off allergies to every known thing. Between her pancreatitis and allergies, what she had left to eat was sick enough to turn the stomach of a starving dog.

None of these things dissuaded her for years from standing on her feet all day in her beauty salon to keep the younger kids in college. And nothing ever squelched her sense of humor or incredible enthusiasm for life. Yet it never seemed to end. Just about the time we thought her physical afflictions might have eased off a little, her woes were aggravated by an auto crash that left Mom with two crushed vertebrae, an arm broken in four places, and months and months of suffering. Although her back finally mended, her arm did not completely mend for some time. For two years, there was nothing but insomnia from pain, weariness from therapy and boredom from partial "house arrest." Add to all that, in the interim there were enough emotional shocks to overload all the systems of a bionic woman. Still, she did not blow her fuse . . . not even when, after all that, she missed a step during a power outage a while later and broke her other arm!

I cannot say I never heard Mom complain of pain and sickness. But never once . . . not even once . . . not in the slightest degree did I hear her rail at God or question His goodness. On the contrary, her faith never flagged as her life lurched from one form of pain to another.

How fortunate are children born to humble parents of aristocratic faith who walk their talk. Though their breed is less than we might hope, it is doubtless greater than we suspect. Children should rise up and call those parents blessed who prize for their family no honor so great as knowing and walking with God. Had living in want been the price of spiritual riches, I have no doubt that my parents would have chosen grinding poverty. Worldly honor gained at the expense of spiritual indigence would for them have been an occasion of sorrow, not celebration. In fact, that question had already been "in court" in our family and the "verdict" was clear.

I have used my parents as models, not because I imagine they represent the pinnacle of discipleship, but because they were just common people whose everyday lives were uncommonly graced with the signature of Christian excellence. They chose not to settle for spiritual mediocrity, but to live beyond the ordinary. They had found a life worth dying for.

Nobody ever heard of them, but I can tell you without exaggeration that their influence indirectly has penetrated the world. To their own way of thinking, they never counted for much. Yet the spark of their spirit ignited their same vision in two sons and a daughter who have in turn spread it to others. Most great fires have small beginnings.

But their posture is by no means unusual. The happy fact that almost everyone can generate similar (or better) examples is welcome evidence that, despite all the flak churches take from their critics (among whom I am one), the spirit of Christian excellence lives even where it languishes. If it is not as intensive as it ought to be, still it is probably more extensive than is thought to be. And the fact that most of us can find exemplars of this attitude so close at hand is a good sign.

The spirit of Christian excellence is like physical strength. It typically displays itself, not all at once, but in little bursts that hint of great reserves. That is why my late father-in-law impressed me so much.

Roy came to Christ at age 47 after a very rough life of drinking, womanizing and brawling. From that point, his life radically changed. In retirement he moved out into the countryside. There for many years he had attended a small country church where, by default, he was a Sunday School teacher. Although he was uneducated and made no pretense of being a gifted teacher, that man in his preparation was more disciplined than a Spartan soldier.

Virtually every day, six days a week, he would spend several hours poring over his Bible, lesson book, commentaries and study resources, sweating out a Sunday School lesson for a mere handful of farm folk, many of whom came to church out of habit and could have cared less. Almost never did the poor man enjoy any of the affirmation most of us require to keep pumped. Yet with indefatigable discipline, the man plodded along like an Oxford scholar, preparing every lesson with the care of a New York lawyer preparing a brief for the Supreme Court. It's laymen like him who frighten me. I fear one day the likes of Roy will rise up to judge some of us who have been given more, but returned less.

But even that did not impress me as much as another side of his Christian character. In a day when people (who have a choice) too readily dump off their spouses, parents and in-laws in nursing homes to die in neglect rather than to be troubled with them, Roy set for me a monumental example.

There came a point when he and Muriel decided that his 90-year-old mother-in-law could no longer safely maintain her private residence. As too often happens these days, most of her own (unbelieving) children turned out (surprise, surprise!) to be unavailable for this duty, at least not for very long. Eventually the whole responsibility fell on Roy and Muriel.

Although they themselves were advancing in years (then in their mid-sixties) and had more financial means than most to afford nursing home care, they refused to subject Mrs. Edelman to that indignity until such time as it might be absolutely necessary. For many of us, that point would have been five years before when she suffered a stroke that left her paralyzed on one side, impaired in her speech capacity and unable to control her private functions.

No son ever loved a mother more than Roy loved his mother-in-law. Until her passing many years back, he was better to her than a son. Not only did he insist on keeping her in his home, but he also shared the vigil of constant, ever-trying care with Muriel, even down to changing the dear soul! Many men would not change their own baby, much less an invalid mother-in-law.

But that is not the half of it. After her stroke the man was a wonder to behold. Each day he spent literally hours with Mrs. Edelman in physical and speech therapy. His incredible patience and compassion helped her reclaim her former physical and speech capacities to a degree that her physicians were amazed. One doctor was stupefied.

"Oh God, I just hope that when I am old somebody will care for me like those people care for that woman," he was overheard exclaiming to a nurse. The marvel in that story is the memory of the kind of man Roy Barnett once was. Thirty years before, if you had wanted to purchase something like my father-in-law in a furniture store, you would have asked for "Early Rambo." This man, before his conversion, was pure

Charles Bronson. He asked no quarter and gave none. He was a man whose nose bore the marks of brawls and billy clubs.

In the personalities of Christian men, one observes in some the gentleness of a lamb, in others the gentleness of a lion. The former, often miscredited to grace, is the product of natural birth; the latter, often obscured by strength, is the product of the new birth. Roy Barnett was a lion gentled by the Spirit of God who cared for his infirmed mother-in-law the way a lioness carries her cub in her jaws. That is spiritual excellence gleaming through the cracks of a Christian character.

Thankfully that sort of selfless charity among Christians is more common than is realized.

One such example cropped up on a ministry trip 30 years ago to the California Bay Area. Just before the evening service, I was seated along with my host on a front row not far from a morbidly obese woman who appeared socially, if not mentally, challenged. Driving away after the service, my friend asked me if I had noticed her. I acknowledged that I had. That woman, he said, was an example of the way his church had opened its heart to the lame, the halt, the sick and the blind. This woman, he explained, besides being obese and a total stranger to personal hygiene, was afflicted with a repulsive skin disease. The combination was socially repelling. Worse than that, however, was the fact that between the folds of fat, the skin was moldy green and riddled with runny sores. The sight and smell of her condition converged to gross out the senses.

Despite all that, one unusual woman, an attractive suburban housewife, a busy mother, a refined person and one comfortable in the lap of success, stepped forward as an unlikely angel of mercy. Besides befriending the castoff, accustomed only to rejection, occasionally she would even take the woman into her own home, counsel her about her social and hygienic habits, bathe her and personally clean out her ugly, ubiquitous sores.

How many of us would have been tempted to ignore “the problem” and hope “it” would go away? Models like that remind me how far I have yet to go. Just about the time I hope I am closing on the standard, some saint in a radical act of outrageous obedience blows my cover. Thank God for those “rabbits” of grace among us who force the pace of us “turtles” who covet the crown of spiritual excellence.

To me, one of the most encouraging aspects of that story was the fact that the woman who rose to the occasion took me completely by surprise. A person I assumed to be ordinary turned out to be heroic and a timely reminder that there are probably many more in the closet just like her.

The spirit of excellence in discipleship may be the exception, but it is far from extinct. The spirit of greatness may not reign in the pews, but it persists in quiet corners. Let us, therefore, beware of an Elijah complex which, loosely translated, laments that after us none is left to take up the torch. Let us not become so focused on the surplus of Balaams and Jezebels in the Church that we distort the reality. Let us not assume that just because the institutional church is not at the top of its game, the Kingdom of God may have to forfeit because so few great players remain on the field to contest the issue.

Spiritual heroism didn’t die with our fathers. The ranks of the Church may be swelled by an overabundance of indulgent spectators, but its roster nevertheless includes a host of obscure, but serious, spiritual athletes. God only knows how many Daniels and Dorcases are lost in the shadows of Christendom, out of sight, but full of fight, walking in the light and standing up for what is right.

I have a friend (I'll call him Tom Smith, a pseudonym) in Scottsdale, Arizona who, among others, renewed my faith in the spirit of discipleship among believing businessmen. Although Tom was at the time quite wealthy, he never let money or success games corrupt his value system. On one occasion he was bringing in a new oil well. At prices per barrel current then, that one gusher would have set anyone up for life in only one day.

One bug-eyed young employee spotted Tom at the site.

"Are you Smith?"

"Yes," Tom answered.

"Sir, how does it feel to be rich?" he wondered as he calculated the profits.

"Son," Tom responded, "that's not very important to me. Now don't get me wrong. This well represents a successful venture and I aimed at that. So it's very satisfying to accomplish what you set out to do. But there is something far more important to me than money."

"What's that?" the young man wondered.

"The most important thing in my life is knowing Jesus Christ as my Savior and Lord. Nothing compares to the day He entered my life."

"That means more to you than this?!" he asked incredulously, as if money were the final solution.

"That's right, son," Tom confirmed.

Lest you imagine that exchange was so much pious froth, let me illustrate how well Tom stuck to his mission, even in the rough and tumble give-no-quarter-take-no-prisoners world of corporate America.

A Christian business friend of Tom's had been trying to recruit him for a board position with a Seattle-based corporation. The opportunity was not only flattering, but also perky and profitable. But in view of the demands of his varied business ventures, Tom declined. Finally his friend tipped his hand and explained his hidden agenda.

"Tom," he pleaded, "I've been trying to reach the president. The guy needs Christ and you're about the only person I know who can go toe-to-toe with him. That board spot is your opening."

"Well," Tom reconsidered, "in that case, I'll make myself available."

Now, for what happens next, you need some context. Tom is what people call a self-made man. Until he was 14 years old, the only home he knew was a tent in the Arizona desert. His father was illiterate and his mother, an invalid. The toughness of those early years combined with an extraordinary measure of innate business sense and years of back-to-back successes to produce a formidable and confident man, not intimidated by any slickered-down, over-educated boardroom wonder boys.

Though Tom is a very handsome and stylish fellow, he wears no airs and tolerates none in others. He'd say "ain't" to the President of the United States and never blush. So, he goes to Seattle to meet with the president of this corporation. He is ushered into a richly paneled and opulently appointed executive suite. There sits the CEO on his "throne" like an oriental monarch receiving a lowly petitioner.

As Tom walks in, the executive is puffing on a cigar out of one side of his mouth, trying to converse with Tom out of the other, while one eye is riveted on a hi-tech TV monitor. Now, Tom comes on as the gentlest of men, and, in fact is. But underneath, he is twisted blue steel. The president was about to find out he was overmatched. Tom had chewed up this type before. He came with a purpose and he did not intend to let this corporate bully boy deny his intentions.

Without a word Tom walks over to the big TV and hits the OFF switch.

"You ain't got enough money in this entire corporation to buy my time. I didn't come up here to watch TV. Now let's go to dinner and talk business."

At dinner, a waiter comes by for the drink orders. Just as the party was about to order, Tom interrupted: "Jist a minute now. Ain't gonna be no drinkin' at this lunch. So you can just forgit about that."

Naturally the group was startled into submission. But Tom can be a force under even normal circumstances. They didn't know what hit them. But that was only the first shock. Round two. Finally the entree. The president and his party dived in like hogs on slop.

"Whoa, jist a minute here! Ain't you guys forgittin' somethun? We haven't thanked our God in heaven for His provision. Let's not act so ungrateful. Let's thank God for this food."

So they pause in embarrassment and extreme discomfort while Tom gives thanks. As we were talking about that incident over dinner one evening, Tom explained his rationale:

> "You see, Jim, those fellows didn't have anything to offer me that I needed. So when I went up there, I asked the Lord to help me show those men a kind of man that they had never seen before."

Mission accomplished, no doubt.

Now, many of us might sincerely question whether that bold approach might be overzealous and even counterproductive. But I suspect Tom knew his target. Somehow contextually his style seemed to me poetically appropriate.

However, my burden is not necessarily to commend it as standard procedure, but to illustrate that a radical disciple is not content to be a nominal Christian. Here was a premier, Lear-Jet businessman who had not lost sight of his Christian identity. He knew how to differentiate who he is from how he earns his bread. Business is what he does for a living, but the living, he does for Christ.

His example reminds me of a discussion about proper and improper methods of evangelism once when I was teaching a pastoral theology class. During that class period, we panned several methods. Afterward, a student came up and made a wise comment, which I have never forgotten:

> "Mr. Andrews, I suppose it's alright to discuss right and wrong ways to evangelize. But in my opinion the one mistake that is worse than any other is to do nothing."

Right! That is precisely the major problem. Some would take exception to Tom's "aggressive" example. But at least he does something, whereas most do virtually nothing.

We can debate about strategy. But God bless men like Tom who know the agenda and won't be deflected or intimidated by Hell or high water. That is the spirit of Christian excellence I am talking about.

You don't have good sheep without good shepherds. Years ago, we had as a visiting lecturer at the seminary where I was then teaching, the wise and able pastor (a 39-year veteran) of a large church in California. In exhorting our students to shepherd the sheep selflessly, he dredged from his pool of pastoral memories a story that I feel illustrates in miniature the remarkable spirit with which he and many other more obscure but faithful leaders, both at home and abroad, continue to lead the flock of God.

A widow lady had invited the pastor and his wife to dinner. She obviously had gone to a great deal of trouble, including fixing a custard pie, known to be his favorite. Later in the meal, after he had been served his dessert, just as he was preparing to dive in, the pastor caught sight of an ominous dark lump just beneath the skin of the pie. Discreet inspection confirmed his worst fear and initial suspicion . . . a big black fly in the pie! Talk about the Battle of the Bulge! What could he do? If he set it aside, he would crush the heart of the poor soul who had lovingly prepared it. If he called attention to it, he would embarrass her beyond belief. The third and final alternative, which he chose---was to open the hatch and let fly.

Tell me that isn't suffering for Jesus' sake! It doesn't matter whether it kills you or just makes you sick, it all comes under that heading. And every day in ways critics never realize, there are hundreds of shepherds out there that nobody knows, expending themselves with a selflessness that only God sees. Extraordinary living in ordinary people. Maybe one of the most encouraging signs for the Church, in my opinion, is the exceptional spiritual caliber of at least some of its youth and young adults. During the fifties, I passed through high school and college in the so-called Bible Belt. Yet until I went to college, I do not recall knowing, even in my church, a single peer whom I would call anything more than a "casual Christian." In college, I did meet a few earnest believers, but very few.

Today, however, despite the encroaching tide of secularization and rampant hedonism, I encounter some of the most radiant and radical young Christians that I have ever seen. Frankly, in some ways (as much as this goes against all conventional wisdom), I believe (for me, at least) it might be easier to come up now, for the simple reason that I see more committed young people today than I ever knew in my youth. My younger daughter, Juli, who attended Wheaton College (in the mid-1980's), told me a story that exemplifies the attitude of some of the new youth I come across.

On some Friday evenings, a sizeable group of Wheaton students, including Juli, would "invade" downtown Chicago and do street evangelism near the historic Water Tower. At that time, the place was a menagerie of fallen humanity, teeming with castoffs and dropouts . . . the eyes ricochet from the wild to the weird to the woeful. One evening, a friend of Juli's, who was a handsome young fellow, obviously well-bred and possessing no particular affinity for filth, struck up a conversation with a street person named Jane, whom many would dismiss coldly as "a dirty bag lady." His hope was to introduce her to the love of Christ.

The next week, he again encountered her there and chatted with her some more. This got to be a weekly ritual. Apparently the "bag lady" saw in this young fellow something from another world that drew her. Instead of Paul looking for her, she began to look for him on Fridays. One evening in the late spring, near the end of school, the group failed to come into Chicago because of college commitments. The next week, however, they were back and Jane, spotting her young college friend, approached him:

"I missed ya last Friday. Looked fer ya, but couldn't find ya."

"No," Paul explained, "we had obligations at school last week and couldn't come in."

Standing not far from an ice cream stand, the lady offered:

"Want some ice cream?"

"Sure," Paul answered acceptingly, with no idea from which grimy sack she might produce some exotic "street" flavor. Luckily, she drafted a handy cohort to purchase a cup at the shop close by. But when the compliant friend returned with the ice cream, Paul's good fortune ran out when the unkempt lady, with practiced nonchalance, dove her unwashed hand down into her greasy bag to retrieve a dirty discard in order to "share" with her new friend. After dividing the "spoils," she then rummaged through her soiled bag for an extra spoon for Paul. No doubt that spoon had seen more teeth than a dentist.

Paul never flinched. Without fuss or hesitation, he dug right in and finished it off like a connoisseur of Haagen-Dazs. When he was done, taking his napkin, he carefully cleaned the second-hand cup and well-travelled spoon with his napkin and handed it back to his lost friend. Why did he do that? Because he understood what it means to be a disciple, his Christian mandate. My daughter had the good sense to eventually marry that young fellow.

For others to live we have to die a little . . . or a lot. And nobody will die a lot when he has never learned to die a little. Some of the young, it seems to me, often have a better grip on that reality than their elders. These indeed are following the contours of Christian excellence, finding the only life worth living and the one life worth dying for. Those who live it are the kind always willing, for the sake of Christ, to lay something on the line. They are never content to offer to the Lord that which costs them nothing (2 Samuel 24:24).

An epitome of that spirit was reported to me by one of our elders concerning an outreach project of his care group. This group, including adults and teenagers, set out one Sunday afternoon for downtown Portland to pass out bottled water and socks to homeless people. One of the guys, Mark, engaged a certain street lady who offered that she was grateful for the socks, but told him what she really needed was some shoes. Mark looked down at hers and asked, "What size do you wear?"

"Nine," she responded.

He paused a minute and then pulled off his own shoes and gave them to her. In his stocking feet, Mark went on his way with the others for the rest of their time on the streets. No big deal, maybe, but it was mid-February!

Little sparks of inspiration can ignite great fires of aspiration. In this chapter, I have hopefully provided some of those little sparks that may just possibly fire your Christian imagination with a vision of a better "you" in Christ. Such vignettes of persons breaking out of the pack of pedestrian "Christianity" and taking their obedience to Christ to the next level always prod me, at least, to pick up my game.

Exactly **how** do we take it to the next level? Well, first, before we can *build up*, we must be sure we've *built down*. Every great edifice, even a great life, must have a great foundation. Let's consider that subject now.

Chapter 9

The Foundations of Christian Excellence

"The magnitude and worth of a building project may be inferred from the scope and strength of its foundations."

Until he more or less retired from the business world, one of my younger brothers, Bernard, had been a CEO of a well-known retail corporation. One day we were talking shop when Bernard told me that, in hiring executives, there were two absolute essentials he looked for: competitiveness and integrity. Other qualifications counted, of course, but those were foundational, he felt, for success in the corporate world.

By the same token, there are certain habits and attributes that are foundational to the formation and expression of Christian excellence in our lives. With that perspective in view, we must now consider some of the underpinnings of excellence.

While we are concerned primarily with the attainment of the Christian ideal, i.e., with being and doing what we *would* be and do *if* we were as we ought to be, it is still germane to keep one eye cocked for the requirements of traditional excellence as well, since our Christian agenda impacts our secular role. Christian standards sometimes pre-commit one to a high level of professional performance. How could one be a sloppy, careless physician and approximate his or her biblical ideals? How could one be an irresponsible attorney, risking or ruining people's resources and reputations through ineptitude, and maintain Christian standards?

The following foundations of excellence relate mostly to the pursuit of spiritual excellence. Many of them, however, are equally essential to the achievement of any other kind of excellence to which we may find ourselves committed in the context of our mandate.

We must capitalize on our *resources.*

Nobody has ever conquered the peak of Everest without two things: commitment and equipment. The same is true for the ascent to the summit of Excellence. Good intentions are not sufficient; one must have adequate provisions also.

All the resources we need for living an exemplary Christian life are available and accessible to us, "seeing that His divine power has granted to us **everything** pertaining to life and godliness through the true knowledge of Him who called us by His own glory and excellence" (2 Peter 1:3). In union with Jesus Christ, we enjoy the mysterious but extraordinary privilege of spiritual participation in the divine nature with all the promises, rights and resources pertaining thereto (2 Peter 1:4). And therein lays the potential for our escape from the ordinary.

No longer do we have an excuse, whatever our natural disadvantages, to be merely average, mindlessly following the herd, when His provisions now invite and enable us to be exceptional. The spiritual "gear" necessary for us to scale the heights of godliness is already in the "storeroom." What remains is for us to go for it.

Yet some of us dare to undertake this expedition ill-prepared for the severe conditions and barriers we will encounter. We are presumptuous, looking within ourselves for reserves, only to discover too late that the flesh, like water, seeks its own level. Failing to heed the apostolic admonition to "be strong in the Lord, and in the strength of His might (Ephesians 6:10)," we are mortified that we stumble so much on the steep path to spiritual excellence.

Actually we ought to be mystified that we don't stumble worse, for there is no way that we can fire the engine of a supernal spirit with fuels of human nature. Our new inner man must be energized from the depots of the Holy Spirit. But that dogma we propagate better than we appropriate.

What are some resources that we commonly overlook in our preparations?

We need regularly to marinate our minds in the Word of God.

The Scriptures function like "pure milk" that enables spiritual infants to "grow in respect to salvation" (1 Peter 2:2). One can have biblical nurture without spiritual growth, but one cannot sustain spiritual growth without biblical nurture. It is a general law, in the words of J. W. Alexander, that "he who is most familiar with [the Word] will become most like it." That is because intimacy with the Word usually signifies an affinity for it that engenders, in the laws of spiritual development, a conformity to it.

How foolish to substitute, as some do, the "junk food" of pop psychology, daily devotional guides or religious paperbacks for a consistent diet of the Word of

God. Let us not forget the difference between a nutritional supplement and a dietary substitute. Like vitamins, some things which serve us well as supplements will never work as substitutes. No amount of theological, psychological or devotional surrogates are equal to the nutritional value of the wisdom and counsel God has imparted in His Word.

The Word serves not only as food to sustain our strength, but also to enlighten our eyes. Hence it acts as a light or compass for our direction. That is the benefit the Psalmist had in mind when he meditated:

> "Thy word have I treasured in my heart
> That I may not sin against Thee"
> (Psalm 119:11).

and . . .

> "From Thy precepts I get understanding;
> Therefore I hate every false way.
> Thy word is a lamp to my feet
> And a light to my path"
> (Psalm 119:104-105).

As a guide in the art of wise living and for discerning truth and error, the Scriptures have no rival. So sure are its precepts, propositions and principles that we can stake our future on them. Nothing else under heaven is so effective in instructing, convicting, correcting and changing servants of God so that they are rendered fit for every work of any worth (2 Timothy 3:16-17).

One reason we have so much babble in the churches is because we have so little of the Bible in our hearts. Formally, it remains the final authority for Christian faith and practice. Functionally, however, for a disturbing number of professing Christians, the Scriptures are more of a sacred relic than a sacred rule in deciding the issues of life. In the end, we do what we want to and find a way to make God appear to consent. Weighed in the scales of excellence, we are found woefully wanting in both spiritual intelligence and moral compliance.

We need to amp up the prayer.

Prayer, as I define it, is worshipful petition. It is not a psychological exercise nor a ceremonial rite. Christian prayer is a royal privilege purchased at the Cross for a blood-bought child of God that licenses us, in the name of Christ, to "draw near with confidence to the throne of grace, that we may receive mercy and find grace to help in time of need" (Hebrews 4:16).

If God knows our needs before we ask, why is it so essential to pray? For one thing, it is a simple issue of obedience. Both by ample biblical precedent and precept we are admonished to pray earnestly and persistently. "Pray without ceasing" is the biblical imperative (1 Thessalonians 5:17, Ephesians 6:18). We cannot ignore that directive and pretend to be submissive. Prayerlessness is therefore a form of faithlessness, which is the root of powerlessness. God helps those who are suppliant, not self-sufficient.

But obedience, sufficient as it is, is not our only reason for practicing the discipline of prayer. Like everything else the Lord imposes as a spiritual duty, it is as much for *our* good as for *His* glory. Prayer not only honors God by acknowledging Him as the Sovereign

Controller of history and Provider of every good thing, but it, in turn, helps us.

How? It strengthens the lifeline that links us to God in Christ, namely, our faith, for we "are protected by the power of God *through faith*" (1 Peter 1:5). Prayer is an important instrument God uses to keep us in the faith and from drifting off into fatal unbelief, as did Israel in the wilderness. For "without faith it is impossible to please Him" (Hebrews 11:6a).

But how does prayer affect our faith?

Prayer not only **indicates** faith by acknowledging His sovereignty and our dependency, but it also **stimulates** hope. The more we pray, the more we find our anxiety reduced by rising anticipation. Like the sun, a biblically founded optimism begins to break through the pessimistic overcast in our hearts, and we see light where once there was only darkness. The reassuring sense that we have done what is right and reverent combines with the indwelling Spirit to swell our confidence that our problem is in good hands.

But prayer also **corroborates** faith, and that reinforces and enriches the original measure. When God acts on some specific petition, we are hardened in our conviction of His presence and power. What once we affirmed by faith, we now confirm by experience. Biblical propositions buttressed by personal exhibitions shore up our faith in the face of doubt.

Finally, prayer **curbs** sin. How?

It not only bolsters our confidence in God's Word, but also influences the way we approach God's throne. I find nothing harder than to pray with a condemning heart. I cannot bluff God. He knows what I know. The red light on the dashboard of my conscience is signaling that something is amiss in my spiritual engine. How can I pretend all is well when an aggrieved Spirit of God is pointing His finger at the flashing light, saying, "Do something about that!"? When my conscience is breached by guilt, my expectancy evaporates under the heat of conviction. If I do not walk in obedience to His Word, I cannot pray in confidence for His blessing. That jibes with the apostle John:

> "Beloved, if our heart does not condemn us, we have confidence before God" (1 John 3:21).

Therefore, I find that prayer has an inhibiting effect on some of my sinful impulses. Feeling the need of divine resources, I fear a condemning conscience that would short-circuit my petitions. Knowing that God is not responsive to those who are rebellious, I lose confidence if I entertain disobedience in my heart.

Apparently Peter had that problem in mind when he cautioned believing husbands to treat their wives in an understanding and honorable way, as fellow heirs of the grace of life, "so that your prayers may not be hindered" (1 Peter 3:7).

We must be *realistic.*

One of the deadly enemies of Christian growth is unchecked perfectionism. By this I mean the tendency to treat anything short of the ideal as failure.

In the spiritual dimension, this personality trait results in theological aberrations and emotional exasperation. Unable to accept the liabilities of the Fall and the limitations of grace on this side of our glorification, the perfectionistic believer flagellates himself mercilessly for every wart on his character and deficit in his conduct. Introspectively, like a diamond appraiser, he turns his heart and actions upside down and inside out, searching for and grimacing over every blemish. Sooner or later, such a person will throw in the towel in frustration, or will foreshorten the "target" in some way or will seek some "wild herb" from the stores of spiritual quackery that promises a quick fix.

There may appear to be a fine line between the complacency that breeds stagnation and a more appropriate resignation to limitation. Actually the difference is more substantial than meets the eye. The former disposition is content with failure in presuming upon grace in the absence of change; the latter is merely patient with failure in depending upon grace to effect change. The first is passive in defeat; the second is persevering.

Some momentous spiritual changes may be simultaneous with our conversion. Later, after severe struggles, other changes may spontaneously combust. But many spiritual defects are very stubborn. Deeply ingrained in the texture of our character, these yield, not by miles and meters at a time, but by inches and millimeters.

We must get reconciled to the reality that we are a people in process. Sanctification ignites at regeneration and its purifying fires burn for the duration. Since we are far from being finished products, we will be troubled by weakness of the flesh down to the wire. We must not indict ourselves with failure for being normal. Remember that achievement of excellence is not matching the standard, but approximating it. And even when we talk of "approximating" the ideal, we must be careful not to think of it in an absolute sense. The approximation that the spirit of excellence requires of us is a proximity that is appropriate to our own circumstances and resources.

To use a physical analogy, proud parents may boast that their 14-month-old son is "walking very well." By what standard? Not by the standard of adolescent or adult walking, but by the criterion of infant walking. We have a sort of pre-existing consensus about the level of physical agility expected of infants at various stages of development. We assess their progress by the ideal appropriate to that class.

So also in spiritual development. There is an absolute ideal: the model of Jesus in His relationship to the will of the Father. When I talk of "approximating" that ideal, allowance has to be made for process. Some are not as far along in their development as others, but then they are not supposed to be. Maturity, as others have noted, is the result of obedience plus time.

Here a legitimate question arises. How far short of the ideal can one come and still qualify for a spirit of Christian excellence? No farther short than time and circumstances beyond our control can excuse.

I simply cannot prevent all interference from the flesh as I try to tune in on a spiritual frequency. Ugly thoughts will intrude even into sacred reflections. Even in our regenerate state we still have a serious hangover from our old life. Such things are not willful concessions to the flesh, but simply involuntary reflexes of it, like the movements of a decapitated snake.

Grace, if appropriated, modifies these with time, but never suppresses them altogether. For our deliverance from the Fall, though an accomplished fact judicially, is a progressive reality experientially. So then, to the extent that the lag between my professed ideals and my actual practice is chronic but correctable, that self-imposed gap represents mediocrity by default.

One can have a spirit of Christian excellence and be immature; one cannot possess it and be indolent. Therefore, in accepting the challenge of Christian excellence, don't take aim at blamelessness (in any absolute sense) but do declare war on spiritual shiftlessness.

We must *focus*.

Excellence, in the words of Lance Morrow (*Time* essay, March 22, 1982), requires a "steady gaze." In that same essay, the author suggested that "the great intellectual flowering of New England in the 19th century (Hawthorne, Emerson, Melville, Thoreau, Longfellow, et al.) resulted in part from "the very thinness of the New England atmosphere, an under-stimulation that made introspection a sort of cultural resource."

Therein, I suggest, lies an important key to the riddle that has often befuddled some of us: "How did our forebears in the ministry accomplish so much in one lifetime?" One reason is that the pace of life was less frenetic in their day, and consequently, their focus was less divided. But I also suspect that the explanation is more than circumstantial; I imagine it was also partially volitional. They not only had better opportunity, but they exercised the good sense to focus themselves, to harness all their energies to limited objectives and to plow behind the concentrated power of narrowed purposes.

In my own case, for example, I feel nothing has so frustrated the flowering of excellence as this stupid vice: the distribution of my energies and talents across too broad a front. As Charles Churchill (*Epistle to William Hogarth*, l. 573) put it:

> "By different methods different men excel;
> But who is he who can do all things well?"

We need to abandon the illusion of omni-competence, for it leads to a fragmentation that only debilitates us and engenders mediocrity.

I think there is more than one reason for fragmentation of focus. Of course, one of the most obvious is the fallacy of activism. Activity and busyness create a cheap illusion of success and feed our ravenous egos. It is a status symbol to be booked up two years in advance. It means I am living in the fast lane. It sends a "message to mother." Someone has wisely discerned that there are "two things that can destroy your ministry: *apathy and opportunity*."

But there is a more **subtle** cause of some of our fragmentation. This is fear. One of my students, discussing this very issue, put it well:

> "I don't want to miss out on anything."

Most of us have not yet managed to completely disengage ourselves from the traditional success orientation of our culture. Our motives are a "mixed multitude." And, because of that (perhaps) unconscious pressure to succeed, we are afraid not to be at home when opportunity comes knocking.

We are like commodity speculators. We want to make it big, but we hesitate to put all our eggs into one basket. We cover our bets and spread our money around the market so that we will be sure to capitalize on whatever action develops. The only trouble with that strategy is that our resources are now spread so thin that our returns are doomed to marginality.

Whatever the reasons, sociological or psychological, that underlie our scatteredness, we must narrow our focus if we would serve God with honor and distinction in an alien environment.

How?

Consider who you are and what your mission is; then start sorting. Carve out of your life all that superfluity of busyness and energy investment that you cannot realistically justify in terms of who you are supposed to *be* and what you are supposed to *do* in Christ. Give priority respectively to those things that are most essential to the vision, and after that, make place for those which contribute to it in a secondary way. Abandon the irrelevant and deny the incompatible.

Just recently a man in our church who is active in city affairs was elected an elder. No sooner had that happened than he was approached about running for the city council. He called me about possibly getting overcommitted. "Nothing is greater," he said, "than the privilege of serving the Lord as an elder in our church. I just wanted to get your advice as my pastor." Right on. He knew he had to focus and did not want to take on too much.

The secret of focusing our lives was well stated in the headline of a newspaper feature article I saw recently:

"Organize, don't agonize!"

That is what most of us need to do. If we take our meaning and mission seriously in Christ, we need to prioritize. To agonize is to paralyze energy; you organize to realize what you visualize. We need to prune our "branches" and get rid of the "suckers" that sap our strength in the service of Christ.

We must embrace *battles.*

Once a student asked me if I would do him a favor. He asked me not to put his grades on his papers. He explained that he had a catch-22 problem. If he got good grades, he got arrogant, and, if he got less than he expected, he got angry. I told him that, although I would be willing to comply with his wishes, I personally felt his request was unwise and self-defeating.

This student, you see, betrayed a spiritually retarding error that hinders the development of our spiritual character. He thought that if he limited the choice factor, that if he could box out the freedom to fail, he could habituate himself to righteousness. He thought the absence of overt sin was equal to the presence of positive righteousness. That is a subtle but serious error that leads to some perverse approaches to excellence regarding what we are supposed to be, i.e., conforming to our Lord Jesus Christ.

Take an infant, for example. We have the absence of disobedience, but we do not have the presence of obedience. And if we could put that child in a box, insulate it with walls of legislation to block out temptation and the freedom to fail, we might keep it from overt sin, but we would not bring it to righteousness, would we?

Why is that?

Because righteousness is not born of social isolation, but of moral selection. Righteousness requires the freedom to make a choice.

What then is the point?

This student did not need a box; he needed a battle. Virtue is not born in a moral vacuum; rather, character is shaped by the hammer of conflict. Let me trace for you the genealogy of character.

Conflicts beget choices, choices beget habits, and habits beget character. Character is not born in a box of rules, but in a battle of choices. Therefore, don't try to structure the opportunity for conflict out of your life. You need the battle.

We need to be pushed gradually to the edge of our limits. Stress, biblically managed, is an asset, not a liability. Among its fringe benefits in both the spiritual and vocational arenas are these:

A. It will smoke you out of your complacency;
B. It will stretch your competence;
C. It will strengthen your confidence.

But some people run from pressure as if it were a python. Yet, the old adage is as true in spiritual things as other things: no pain, no gain. Strength is the offspring of stress.

We need *role models*.

By having models, I mean you need to expose yourself as much as possible to those people and things that exemplify and embody the spirit of excellence. Let me make a few observations about the value of role models.

In the first place, models tend to motivate us. As Proverbs (27:17) says:

> "As iron sharpens iron, so man sharpens man."

Most exceptional people have adopted their own special role models who exemplify qualities or dimensions of excellence that they admire. These role models inspire us to greater effort to cultivate those qualities when we are exposed to them. Cicero had Demosthenes as his model. Caesar had Alexander the Great as his. Our role models tend to measure us and, having measured us, spur us to greater effort to measure up.

Secondly, our models tend to mold us. Proverbs (13:20) says:

> "He who walks with wise men will be wise."

It seems to be a general truth that we tend to become like what we love; we tend to become what we think about. You are what you think:

> "Finally, my brethren, whatever is true, whatever is honorable, whatever is right, whatever is pure, whatever is lovely, whatever is of good repute, if there is any excellence and if anything worthy of praise, let your mind dwell on these things" (Philippians 4:8).

Perhaps the most impressive parable of this reality in the American literature I know is Nathaniel Hawthorne's story of "The Great Stone Face."

Hawthorne tells of a young boy enchanted by the character carved by nature in the lines of a great stone face protruding from a nearby mountain. All his life the youth pondered intently the character in that face with wonder and awe. Gradually and imperceptibly, the character of the Great Stone Face began to imprint the character of the boy, until at last Ernest bore its image. As I've said, our models tend to mold us. Let me make some final comments about the use of role models.

First, make sure you have good role models both in men and in things. The principle that "a servant can rise no higher than his master" is involved here. You will hit no higher than you aim; you will reach no higher than you stretch.

Second, be sure you have a sufficient number of role models. Again Charles Churchill's lines are to the point:

> "By different methods, different men excel;
> But who is he who can do all things well?"

Third, be sure you measure all models by the Ultimate Model, the only One who "does all things well." There are times when the excellence of our models blinds us to their edges and excesses, and there are other times when we unwittingly mistake their errors for their excellence. Only as we train ourselves to test our mortal models by the Master Model, can we check ourselves.

We must be *teachable.*

Criticism from any source is useful in the ascent to excellence.

Henry Ward Beecher, according to Ralph Turnbull in *The Minister's Obstacles*, "testified to one great truth in his riper years, that as much as he owed to himself, he owed still more to his enemies. His friends, he said, never saw his faults and, if his enemies exaggerated them, nevertheless they compelled him to see them."

Nobody has put it better than Minucius, Fabius' Master of the Horse, in Livy's account of *The War with Hannibal* (Penguin Classics, p. 128):

> "I have often heard that the best man is he who can give good counsel; the next best is he who is ready to obey the good counsel of another. Long last comes the fool who is too ignorant to do either."

Excellence of any kind requires the ability to profit from criticism and reproof. Unfortunately, some of us are so insecure that we don't invite criticism, and so proud that we reflexively reject it even when we receive it. Raw ability is a more common commodity than teachability.

We need *self-control.*

First, you need to control your time.

The ability to manage time wisely has always been an attribute of men of achievement. Napoleon is reported to have guarded his time so carefully that he once claimed no one would ever be able to accuse him of wasting a minute.

According to Plutarch (*Lives of the Noble Grecians and Romans)*, Julius Caesar in his Gallic campaigns used to ride into battle with a secretary on either flank, dictating his correspondence and commentaries.

If God cannot trust us with our minutes, why should He trust us with His gifts? He who loses the battle of the minutes loses the war against mediocrity. But, if they are disciplined and wisely deployed, our minutes can storm and subdue the most stubborn walls of resistance to our labors. Remember that in your youth, time is on your side. I hope that in your maturity it may not be on your conscience.

Second, you must have control of your passions.

Some will never excel, not for lack of capacity, but for lack of control. Like Reuben, they shall not have pre-eminence because they are "uncontrolled as water" (Genesis 49:4). How many times have blind and mindless surrenders to lust, to anger, to appetite and to pleasure aborted the assault on excellence!

Let us take our cue from the Apostle Paul himself who acknowledged the constant need for vigilance over our passions when he testified in 1 Corinthians 9:27:

> "I buffet my body and make it my slave, lest possibly, after I have preached to others, I myself should be disqualified."

Some of us assume too little responsibility for our **external** control. For example, only the Spirit of God can keep me from coveting, but I can keep myself from stealing. Only the Spirit of God can control my lusting, but I can keep myself out of the wrong bed. We must learn to accept more responsibility for our breakdowns! As has been said, "You cannot keep a bird from flying over your head, but you can keep it from building a nest in your hair."

Sometimes pure pagans exhibit far more self-control for less noble causes than do we Christians, who are endowed with the Spirit of God, for the prize of the high calling of God in Jesus Christ. Witness, for example, the remarkable control evinced in the character of Scipio Africanus, the young Roman general who defeated the great Hannibal, when Scipio rebuked his young Numidian ally, Masinissa, for an outbreak of blind passion. Drawing Masinissa aside, Scipio said:

> "I believe that it was because you saw some good in me that you came to me first in Spain to win my friendship, and afterwards here in Africa put yourself and all your hopes into my hands. But of the virtues which might have made you wise to seek my friendship, there is none on which I should have prided myself as much as on self-control and superiority to the lusts of the flesh. How I wish, Masinissa, you had added this to your other excellent qualities! Believe me, for young men like us there is no peril from an armed foe to be compared with the peril of being surrounded with opportunities for sensual enjoyment. The man who has tamed and bridled the wild horses of lust has won himself more honor and a greater victory than is ours by the defeat of Syphax . . . Be master of yourself: do not spoil many fine qualities by one defect, nor ruin our gratitude for all your services

> by a fault so infinitely graver than its cause" (Livy, *The War with Hannibal*, 30:14).

We must *persevere.*

Let me explain why perseverance is so essential in the ascent to the peak of excellence.

First, great achievements, spiritual or otherwise, usually require great effort. Do not recoil from that word as if it were legalistic. The Scriptures know nothing of a passive spirituality.

Peter is quite plain about the place of human effort in the scheme of sanctification by grace when he admonishes believers:

> ". . . applying all diligence, in your faith supply moral excellence, and in your moral excellence, knowledge; and in your knowledge, self-control, and in your self-control, perseverance, and in your perseverance, godliness; and in your godliness, brotherly kindness, and in your brotherly kindness, Christian love" (2 Peter 1:5b-7).

Peter ***assumes*** the provisions of grace ["everything necessary for life and godliness" v.3] and demands that we cooperate with its scheme. That scheme enlists our cooperation. Paul appeals for the same holy alliance of divine input with human output (Philippians 2:12-13).

It has been well said that "nothing is such an obstacle to the production of excellence as the power of producing what is good with ease and rapidity" (John Aiken, *Christianity Today*). A great artist was reportedly asked how long it took him to paint a certain masterpiece. He replied, "All my life." Genius is 99%

perspiration and 1% perspicacity: "Genius is an infinite capacity for taking pains."

Second, great achievers usually have to surmount great obstacles.

Demosthenes, the peerless Greek orator, comes to mind. He so aspired to excellence in rhetoric that, to overcome a serious speech impediment, he used to practice speaking for hours on end with smooth rocks in his mouth.

One of the all-time inspirational examples of determination in the face of adversity was Shun Fujimoto of Japan, a gymnast in the 1976 Montreal Olympic Games. According to *Time* magazine:

> "During his floor exercise, Fujimoto fractured his right leg. But with the Japanese in contention for a team gold medal, he refused to give up. Fitted with a plastic cast from hip to toe, he somehow competed in the ring exercise and achieved the highest score of his life. He finished with a triple somersault and twist that doomed him to excruciating pain when he landed. But he executed it flawlessly, and fearlessly and maintained his balance long enough to clinch the gold for his team before his leg crumpled grotesquely beneath him.
>
> 'It is beyond my comprehension,' said an Olympic doctor who treated Fujimoto, 'how he could land without collapsing in screams. What a man.'

> 'Yes, the pain shot through me like a knife,' said Fujimoto. 'It brought tears to my eyes. But now I have a gold medal, and the pain is gone.'"

Dr. Earl Radmacher, former president of Western Seminary, once handed me this quote after one of my chapel messages on this subject:

> "The test of your character is what it takes to stop you."

A famous track coach and husband of a great Olympian always told his daughter, as she related on a TV special, "Champions are not made by successes but by obstacles."

All these things in my opinion are crucial to the pursuit of spiritual excellence. But the cornerstone remains to be considered. Without it any pursuit of Christian excellence would be in vain.

Chapter 10

The Cornerstone of Christian Excellence

"For me to live is Christ and to die is gain" (Phil 1:21).

In learned discussion, one sometimes encounters the Latin phrase *"sine qua non."* It means literally "without which nothing." Usually it refers to some feature or attribute of a thing upon which everything else hinges. Without that element, the critical core is absent.

Christ-centeredness is the *sine qua non* of discipleship. And it is both the means and the end of Christian excellence.

If that seems contradictory, it is only apparently so. An analogy is the area of health. Physical fitness is at once the goal of good health habits and also a means of achieving it. In other words, fitness in large measure defines healthfulness, but also engenders it. In the same way, Christ-centeredness develops what it defines, namely, spiritual excellence.

Unfortunately, indiscriminate usage has milked the concept of "Christ-centeredness" of much of its idea-power. Overwork has reduced it from priceless cachet to a cheap cliché. Now, I fear, familiarity has bred apathy. The idea is too familiar to sneak meaningfully past our ear-gate---too anemic to break through our cynicism and arrest the imagination. "Christ-centeredness" suffers from meaning inflation. That is, the notion lacks the buying power, meaning-wise, that it used to. Just as it is with our dollars, so it is with our words. Some are less informational than they used to be.

Take, for example, the entertainment word, "star." That status has been so loosely employed over the years that it carries less weight all the time. Nowadays it seems everyone on TV is a "star." So now, to get across the fact that someone is *really* a star, we prop up the original word with "super" [star]. Same in the sports world.

So, what has happened to other religious words and phrases has also affected our evangelical cliché, "Christ-centered." Loose use has eroded the radicalism of the idea. How many churches, schools and ministries co-opt the phrase as an evangelical buzzword to accredit themselves with their publics as a spiritual-minded entity or individual who is interested in more than parochial institutional or intellectual concerns? Of course, that is all to the good as far as it goes, but "Christ-centeredness" is a mindset far deeper, more radical, much riskier and more self-denying than all that.

So we either can discard the phrase for a fresh alternative or we can try to resuscitate this one. I have opted for the latter course since I believe "Christocentric" describes more incisively the whole mental habit we disciples are called to exhibit.

True, the word appears nowhere in the New Testament, but then neither does "trinity." The mere absence of a term, as most of us know well, in no way refutes the presence of an idea. Many of the labels (e.g., dualism, idealism, nominalism, etc.) that we use to describe the notions of the ancient philosophers, they themselves never used to describe their own philosophies. Still, if those thinkers were around today, they no doubt would consent to the accuracy of the categories into which we have put their thought. And so too, we have the right to coin words to categorize biblical ideas that lack a pithy descriptor.

But where in the New Testament does that spiritual fixation break through most impressively? Since we have more autobiographical material from the hand of Paul than any other New Testament figure, it is natural that he should be our most likely model of the Christocentric spirit that should possess us all. And indeed, he is the epitome of the ideal.

Few men have ever been so consumed with Christ as this completed Jew. His attitude exemplifies as well as any on record what it means to be "centered" on Jesus Christ. Here was a man who buttoned his shirt one hole at a time just like we do and yet, unlike most of us, served Christ so single-mindedly that he almost single-handedly changed the face of the Greco-Roman world and the course of history. It's not that Paul did it under his own power, but rather through his devotion, and so God's power, reached its perfection in a mortal way.

Few of Paul's writings are as personal as the Philippian epistle. It is there as much as any other place that he lays bare his heartstrings. We learn what drives the man, what fixes his agenda, what turns his engines!

Had these thoughts been aired in comfortable circumstances we might have been tempted to blow them off. After all, pious talk is cheap when one has never gone toe-to-toe with pain and privation. It's easy to be a "tiger" in the absence of "poachers" who want to take your hide. Or, only when shots start getting fired do we discover who the real Marines are.

This epistle was written "under fire." A man whose heart was relatively as pure as driven snow, so to speak, was incarcerated as a criminal and public enemy in a Roman prison. The defamation of character alone would have cooked my spirit. What his physical conditions and trials were, we don't know precisely. You can be sure it wasn't a vacation spot with resort conditions. You can bet nobody in the Roman world envied his accommodations or his prospects. Roman justice, true, was a little ahead of its time (where *citizens* were concerned). Even so, you can believe that even a day in a Roman prison was one you would rather forget. Even today, prison is a nightmare, and since the days of the Caesars, things for inmates have improved dramatically, if that tells us anything.

That perspective renders Paul's sentiments in Philippians 1:12-21 even more remarkable. When God is adding, it's easy to froth; when He is subtracting, it's easier to fret. But this man is not smoldering with resentment about all the people who flaked out on him, is not sulking or pouting about his disappointment with God. He is not even asking people to pray that he will be released from his humiliating confinement. Rather, he is effusing with joy and excitement about how the power of God has turned his chains to the advantage of the Gospel. His tone is thoroughly triumphant in tribulation. Whatever afflictions prison conditions may have imposed, Paul ignores, for his life is mastered by a higher purpose and priority than his personal comfort.

His thinking is fixated, not on his bonds as such, but rather on the gains Christ has made through his chains (verses 12-14). From the prison the Gospel has penetrated even the palace of the emperor through the leavening influence of his Praetorian guards (verse 13).

And, ironically, he reports, instead of his incarceration intimidating the brethren outside, it has only served to embolden them to take up the slack. The preaching of the Gospel of Christ has not been hindered, but literally multiplied by his persecution (verse 14).

Of course, Paul concedes, not everyone who has stepped into the void created by his apostolic absence has been as highly motivated as others in preaching Christ. Some preach Christ for better reasons, some for worse. There are actually those who, as envious rivals of Paul, preach the Gospel in hope of supplanting Paul and causing him distress by their inroads into his "turf" of influence during his absence.

What is his reaction to these things? As the Apostle bares his feelings, his single-minded Christ-centeredness bursts through like the sun at high noon. His response establishes the radical meaning of Christ-centeredness for all time.

It shines through, first of all, in his **solitary ambition in life, namely, to magnify Christ.** To bring out his spirit more clearly, let me paraphrase his answer (vss.15-21):

> "What is my response to these things? Shall I get bent out of shape because some preach Christ from such offensive motives? That is, shall I allow the proclamation of Christ to be prostituted by allowing it to degenerate into a rivalry over influence in the Church? No, I refuse to fall into that trap! On the contrary, I rejoice that Christ is proclaimed. That is my passion and my interest. If He is preached, if His cause is enhanced, my cause is advanced. May their motives change, but I say let their message remain!

This attitude is the appropriate one *and* the only one that, along with your prayers and the enablement of the Holy Spirit, will further my consuming ambition. It is my earnest expectation and desire that with all boldness, Christ shall even now, as always, be exalted in my body, whether by life or by death. With the help of God I don't want to do anything inconsistent with that goal. For in my mind, Christ is the measure of everything. The meaning of living is Christ, and the advantage of dying is to be with Him. He is the focus of my whole being, whether living or dying."

William Barclay has captured the lesson well:

"All that mattered to him [Paul] was that Christ was preached. All too often we resent it because someone else gains prominence or a credit or a prestige which we do not receive. All too often we regard a man as an enemy because he has expressed some criticism of us or of our methods. All too often we think a man can do no good because he does not do things our way. . . . Paul is a great example. He was cleansed of self; he had lifted the matter beyond all personalities; all that mattered was that Christ was preached."

Paul's ambition was singular:

"Let Christ be magnified in my person."

It was also unconditional: Let it happen on whatever terms You deem necessary, he says in effect.

We take ourselves too much for granted. I think most of us assume that we are more committed than we are. Do you consider yourself Christ-centered?

Could you honestly say that if it would magnify Christ more, you would prefer imprisonment to liberty, poverty to wealth, anonymity to notoriety, singleness to companionship, sickness to health, or the appearance of failure to the trappings of success? Could you sincerely ask God to arrange the alternative most conducive to the glory of Christ through your life?

Paul could. And so could many others, ancient and modern, who have walked in his radical steps. Jesus Christ has never lacked for choice servants who, as someone said, "long for their bodies to be theaters in which the glory of Christ is displayed." Taking Paul as our standard, no believer has any valid claim to Christocentricity who cannot and does not make that petition his standing prayer.

Secondly, the Apostle's Christocentric spirit rings out in his **evaluation of Christ** (v.21):

> "For me to live is Christ and to die is gain."

But what does that really mean? For a Christocentric person like Paul, it means, for one thing, that Christ is the meaning of life. John Eadie elaborated the Apostle's sentiment this way:

> "For me to live is Christ, the preaching of Christ is the business of my life; the presence of Christ, the cheer of my life; the image of Christ, the crown of my life; the spirit of Christ, the life of

> my life; the love of Christ, the power of my life; the will of Christ, the law of my life; the glory of Christ, the end of my life."

However, Paul also meant that Christ was the measure of life. Our humanistic culture concurs with Protagoras that man is the measure of all things, i.e., that the worth of anything is determined by its value to man as the center of intelligent existence.

For the Christ-centered man, the standard of worth is not man, but Christ. He is the measure of all things. The worth of anything is proportionate to its value in glorifying and enjoying Him. Life is valued because of the opportunity to proclaim Him. Death is valued because of the opportunity to live in His presence.

How does a Christocentric person measure people? By their relationship to Christ.

How does a Christocentric person measure things? By their usefulness in serving Christ.

How does a Christocentric person measure experiences? By their compatibility with His purposes and consistency with His character.

This attribute (Christ-centeredness) then, is the capstone of spiritual excellence, a spirit which in a great way defines it, and yet one which also develops it.

In summary, to be Christocentric is to be so fixated on Christ that life, in all its dimensions, is a holy conspiracy to magnify Him. It is to find in Jesus our meaning, our mission and our Master. Since He expended His all in our behalf, we conclude that He is entitled to our all in His behalf. Our living should imitate His dying. Therefore, withdrawing all claim to personal rights and a private life, we put our lives on divine consignment. We offer ourselves as a sacrifice upon the altar of His service. Time, talents, resources, relations, assets over which once we claimed jealous ownership, now we see simply as a sacred stewardship entrusted to us for investment in His glory. Whereas once I measured my life by what I got out of it, now I measure it by what *He* gets out of it.

There are, as I like to say, three kinds of lives: those that expire without the knowledge of Christ, those that transpire without making much difference for Christ and those that light a fire for the glory of Christ. The difference is the spirit of uncompromising discipleship. For Paul this was the life worth dying for.

Know, then, that real excellence is a live option for **you**. It is within your reach if you stretch by grace. Any believer can be exceptional. The ordinary person can be extraordinary in the ways that count. An obscure man can be outstanding in the midst of anonymity, for excellence is simply an all-out assault on the peak of your potential as a child of God.

This quest requires no special input. All that is essential, God has put in trust for us. What it does require on our part is extraordinary output. Nothing but our own indolence can deny us access to true excellence. For the climb before us, we might appropriate a part of Longfellow's summons:

> "We have not wings, we cannot soar;
> But we have feet to scale and climb
> By slow degrees, by more and more,
> The cloudy summits of our time.

The mighty pyramids of stone
That wedge-like cleave the desert airs,
When nearer seen, and better known,
Are but gigantic flights of stairs.

The distant mountains, that uprear
Their solid bastions to the skies,
Are crossed by pathways, that appear
As we to higher levels rise.

The heights by great men reached and kept
Were not attained by sudden flight,
But they, while their companions slept,
Were toiling upward in the night.

Standing on what too long we bore
With shoulders bent and downcast eyes,
We may discern--unseen before--
A path to higher destinies,

Nor deem the irrevocable Past
As wholly wasted, wholly vain,
If, rising on its wrecks, at last
To something nobler we attain."

-The Ladder of St. Augustine

If any incentive is needed, think of the monumental dignity that the spirit of excellence confers on the most humble life! The vicissitudes of life can strip one of almost every dignity but this one distinction. No matter what our personal limitations, no matter how inferior our social station, a spirit of Christian excellence sets one apart as beyond the ordinary. It crowns our character with a royal touch that no humiliation can obscure.

True nobility is not a matter of title or pedigree. It is a matter of character. As Graham Scroggie wrote:

> "Some called kings are curs.
> All kings are not crowned;
> All those crowned are not kings.
> Some potentates are pygmies;
> Many servants are sovereigns."

Surely it is only befitting that those who have been given "the power to become the children of God" (John 1:12) should strive steadfastly to cultivate a character that corresponds with their royal pedigree in Christ. Such a godly pursuit is out of this world and totally beyond the ordinary in the field of human endeavors. Only that relentless quest yields a life worth dying for, and therein one discovers the radical meaning of Christian excellence.

No more fitting conclusion to this book comes to mind than the inspiring sentiment expressed in that poem (*I'd Rather Have Jesus*) by Rhea Miller and famously set to music by the late George Beverly Shea:

> I'd rather have Jesus than silver or gold;
> I'd rather be His than have riches untold;
> I'd rather have Jesus than houses or lands;
> I'd rather be led by His nail-pierced hand
>
> Refrain: Than to be the king of a vast domain
> And be held in sin's dread sway;
> I'd rather have Jesus than anything
> This world affords today.

I'd rather have Jesus than men's applause;
I'd rather be faithful to His dear cause;
I'd rather have Jesus than worldwide fame;
I'd rather be true to His holy name

Refrain

He's fairer than lilies of rarest bloom;
He's sweeter than honey from out of the comb;
He's all that my hungering spirit needs;
I'd rather have Jesus and let Him lead

Refrain

The Notion of Excellence in the Streets and in the Scriptures

This appendix is one of those "in case anybody is interested" add-ons. Certainly, where the Bible is concerned, some will be interested, I'm sure. Perhaps others may find my modestly analytical breakdown of the way the streets talk about excellence useful for some purpose.

In the former case, as one who strives to be a "radical Biblicist," I would like never to be (justly) accused of holding a religious "philosophy" not grounded in revelation. Thus, somewhere it seemed appropriate to more or less survey what the Bible has to say on the subject explicitly or implicitly. Yet, inserting a chapter of this kind of material in the main body of the book, especially one that might seem boringly abstract, or in the case of scriptural usage, read a bit like an annotated concordance, seemed to just beg the reader to stop right there.

So, for whatever it's worth, that is my rationale for reserving this material as an appendix.

In the streets, so to speak, *excellence* is obviously an evaluative term like good or bad, or big or little. The measuring stick of excellence in any given situation may be absolute or relative. Then, too, what is considered "excellent" may show up either in: 1) the quality of our *pursuit or process*, or 2) the quality of the *product* or *outcome* . . . or both. It is important to bear these distinctions in mind.

If the criterion is the fixed or more absolute standard, then excellence comes down to *approximating the ideal* (in a given type of endeavor). An "ideal" answers to the highest conception of a thing. Excellence in this sense is measured by the way we, or some experts, feel is the way something would be when it is as it ought to be. Excellence in this absolute paradigm is not achieved merely by surpassing others, but depends on achieving proximity to the ideal.

Someone (I forget who) had this definition in mind when he said:

> "An enterprise is excellent when it is true to its own ideals."

Professional coaches, for instance, have a fairly consistent mental model of the ideal skills they would like to see in an NBA basketball player---that is, the ideal player. In the 1980's, Michael Jordan approximated that ideal in terms of basketball skills and competitive mentality. Justly, he is pronounced by most as one of the greatest ever to play the game. He excelled in terms of approximating the mental ideal.

When I was still in academia, a committee chairman once submitted a report to me. I liked it very much. His committee had done its homework. They had crystallized the issues, stated their assumptions, made their recommendations, and justified them with evidence and solid argumentation. Their position was judicious, balanced, and for the most part, clearly stated. I pronounced the report "excellent." My standard was an absolute criterion. I measured it, not by previous standards, but rather by my own mental model of what such a report ought to be. In my mind, there was an almost Platonic ideal. I felt the committee's work approximated that standard.

But there is another way to judge something or someone to be excellent. If one measures the quality of any endeavor by the relative standard of previous performances, then excellence amounts to *surpassing the prevailing norm.*

The prevailing norm is not what is ideal, but what is ordinary or customary. The prevailing norm is what we have come to expect of ourselves and others in a given situation.

Maybe that norm is simply an informal mental standard based on my experience of what is normally expected and accepted. Or, that norm may be based upon some codified or formal standard for a given function. That standard may be well short of my highest conception of things in this category, but contextually, it is the best that one normally has the right to expect.

A prison warden might describe the conduct of a convict doing time as "excellent." Most likely he means by the prison standard, i.e., by the norms of that violent, hate-filled, authority-despising context.

Now these theoretical definitions are not conflicting, but complementary. They represent an attempt to account for two valid perspectives in judging excellence. One is more absolute and the other more relative. The second is more fluid, simply because its criterion is more changeable.

Additionally, sometimes when we pronounce something "excellent," what we have in mind is not the outcome or product (which might have been well short of the ideal) but the heroic effort someone put forth. It is not the approximation of an ideal that we praise, but the relentless pursuit of it.

The Concept of Excellence in the Bible

In biblical usage, the notion of "excellence" is consistent with these perspectives. In the New American Standard (NASB) and King James (KJV) versions of the Bible, more than 35 Hebrew and Greek words are translated "excel." All that means is that the translators felt that, in the original texts, Hebrew and Greek terms appear which correspond to our popular or generic notions of "excellence." (All references listed in this chapter are from the NASB unless otherwise stated.)

Old Testament Usage

Take, for example, the Hebrew verb *alah*. Its primary meaning is simply *to go up, ascend or climb*. From that root notion, this verb, like other words, acquires secondary or metaphorical meanings, depending on context, which grow naturally out of its base denotation. Thus *alah* could quite easily extend its semantic range to include the idea of "excelling." And that is precisely the way it is used in Proverbs 31:29, where the husband praises his good wife:

> "Many daughters have done nobly, but you <u>excel</u> (*alah*) them all."

That is, she has gone up, ascended or climbed above others. This is "excellence" in both the sense of surpassing the prevailing norms, but also going further and approximating the Hebrew ideal of womanhood.

In Jeremiah 5:28, where the prophet is indicting the nation, Jeremiah describes corrupt men among them as persons who "excel in deeds of wickedness." The Hebrew word is *abar.* The primary meaning of the verb is "pass over, through, by, pass on." Those whom the prophet condemns pass over or surpass the normal restraints that might inhibit other evildoers. In other words, they are evil to excess, that is, well beyond the ordinary.

Of course, in the Old Testament, this attribute of excellence is ascribed to God, but not always by the same Hebrew terminology. In Psalm 150:2 the poet summons His worshipers to "praise Him according to His excellent (*rob*) greatness." The Hebrew word *rob,* here translated "excellent," denotes multitude, abundance or greatness. Thus the psalmist extols the greatness of His greatness, i.e., the kaleidoscopic abundance of it. God is transcendent . . . surpassing the great in greatness.

In 1 Kings 4:30, the KJV says "Solomon's wisdom excelled (*rabah*) the wisdom" of the learned among the surrounding nations. The verb has the residual idea of being or becoming much, many or great. The grammatical structure requires a comparative rendering of the verb form. Hence, the wisdom of Solomon "excelled" in the sense that it exceeded or surpassed the norm of his sage contemporaries.

Daniel (6:3) began distinguishing himself among the commissioners and satraps of Darius because (KJV) "an excellent (*yattir*) spirit was in him." The adjective is a Chaldean word that signifies very great, abundant or preeminent. Appropriately, the NASB translates the original in this place with the English word "extraordinary." Here "excellent" amounts to approximating the ideal spirit.

In Psalm 148:13, the KJV translates it "His name alone is excellent (*sagab*) . . ." The NASB translates the same predicate adjective as "exalted." The verb, according to Brown, Driver and Briggs, means "to be (inaccessibly) high." His renown is above and beyond all rivals. His reputation has no equal. What He is surpasses all. That "surpassing" notion is embedded in it.

Ruth is acknowledged by Boaz, her kinsman redeemer, as one who is reputed around the city of Bethlehem as "a woman of excellence (*chayil*)" [Ruth 3:11]. The original word includes in its semantic field the ideas of strength, efficiency, ability or wealth. Context has to determine which notion is in view. Here, no doubt, the point is that Ruth is a woman of remarkable (beyond the ordinary) strength of character. The narrative features her strength in her uncommon spirit and her extraordinary loyalty. In this case, the usage is more consistent with the absolute standard. Ruth approximates the ideal in feminine character.

These are some of the Old Testament terms rendered "excellent" (or one of its cognate forms) in either the NASB or the KJV. Most of the other Old Testament words that include the notion of excellence in their field of meaning also seem to entail root ideas similar to these. So, all these Hebrew terms are freighted with the connotation of surpassing the ordinary in some relative way or approximating the ideal. Their subjects are in some way viewed as superior in strength, power, beauty, capacity, exaltedness, and, in one case, even wickedness.

New Testament Usage

A survey of New Testament words translated by some cognate of our English term "excellence" follows the same pattern. For example, in 1 Thessalonians 4, we have the Greek verb *perisseuo* used twice:

> " . . . you have received from us instruction as to how you ought to walk and please God . . . , that you may excel (*perisseuo*) still more" (v.1).

Again, the idea of surpassing the prevailing spiritual norm blends nicely with approximating the Christian moral ideal.

Later in the same passage, where the Apostle commends the church for practicing love toward all the brethren in Macedonia, he urges them "to excel (*perisseuo*) still more" (v.10). That Greek verb means to be over and above, to abound. Once again, the relative and absolute standards merge.

Another verb used for excellence in the New Testament is *diaphero* (and its adjective cognate, *diaphoros*). The verb form appears in Philippians 1:10, where Paul prays that the Philippians "may approve the things that are excellent." That verb conveys the notion of carrying across or carrying through (certain markers). From that root idea, it came to be used of things that exceeded or surpassed other things, that is, differed from them. So the Apostle's appeal is for them to elect those values and behaviors that differ from the old order, i.e., values and behaviors that are superior, or rise above, or surpass the worldly standard not only in degree, but in kind.

From the idea of "different" in the sense of superior, we easily pass to the notion of preeminence. Thus in Hebrews 1:4 and 8:6, respectively, the writer refers to our Lord as having "inherited a more excellent (*diaphoros*) name" than the angels, and as having "obtained a more excellent (*diaphoros*) ministry than Aaron." Again, the basic idea in both cases is a *surpassing* difference.

In 1 Corinthians 12:31, the Apostle says:

> "And I show you a still more excellent (*hyperbole*) way [i.e., to minister to and to edify the Church]."

That original word comes from the verb *hyperballo*. It means to go beyond, to surpass, to outdo. In the noun form, in which we find it here, the word implies a throwing beyond (others). By a very natural passage, it then comes to mean superiority or excess. As in other cases, the nuance that applies in any particular case depends on the context.

Now, among the New Testament words bearing the sense of excellence, some speak of "excellence" in the more absolute sense of approximating (or exemplifying) an ideal. The word that is used most often in the New Testament (5 times) in the sense of excellence is *arete*. It means goodness or excellence of any kind. Of all the Hebrew and Greek words meaning "excellence," this is one of the few that doesn't have a root idea of exceeding or surpassing in some way. Rather, it seems to have in view a fixed ideal of virtue. God embodies this virtue or excellence and believers ought to seek to emulate it by grace.

In the New Testament, the term *arete* is twice applied to God. Peter speaks of Him "who called us by His own glory and excellence (2 Peter 1:3b). In 1 Peter 2:9, the Apostle reminds us of God's purpose, i.e., "that you might proclaim the excellencies of Him who has called you out of darkness into His marvelous light." In both cases, God is the repository of virtue. Obviously, in the case of God, He does not merely approximate virtue or excellence, but by His very nature, He embodies and defines the ideal.

In Philippians 4:8 believers are admonished:

> "Finally, brethren, whatever is true, whatever is honorable, whatever is right, whatever is pure, whatever is lovely, whatever is of good repute, if there is any excellence and anything worthy of praise, let your mind dwell on these things."

Moral excellence is assumed to be the sense of that word also in 2 Peter 1:5, where the NASB uses that very rendering:

> ". . . in your faith supply moral excellence, and in your moral excellence, knowledge."

In both instances, the Apostle exhorts believers to strive to close in on the moral ideal.

Finally there is the Greek word *kalos*, which means beautiful, honorable or noble. It is translated "excellent" in 1 Peter 2:12 ("keep your behavior excellent among the Gentiles"). Again, a moral ideal is the object of pursuit.

While this list of Greek and Hebrew terms used for excellence in the NASB and KJV is not exhaustive, it is indeed representative.

Summary of the Data

A sense of *transcendence* (of a prevailing norm) seems to run through the majority of the biblical terms. To our English translators, the idea of surpassing others, or going beyond the normal or exceeding a standard corresponded to the English notion of excelling. Whenever they encountered Hebrew or Greeks words with those connotations, the translators often chose the idea of "excellence" to express it.

Likewise, they view excellence in the other sense of correspondence to an ideal. The Greek words *arete* and *kalos* especially fit this conception.

So, we can conclude that, in biblical as well as popular usage, excellence denotes *superiority* in some respect.

One can be superior merely in the sense that one exceeds others in some way. For example, I might run faster than my mother, but still be less than mediocre by ideal standards for a man my age.

One can also be superior in a more absolute sense. After a medical checkup, my doctor may pronounce me in superior health. He is not thinking necessarily of the prevailing norm---I could be in a nursing home. If that is what he meant, I could be in marginal health and still be better off than those around me. More likely he has in mind an ideal medical standard for any male my age. By that criterion, he considers my physical condition "superior."

To excel then, is (from a relative standpoint) *to surpass the usual standard.* It is to be superior to the norm. It is to transcend the ordinary.

Or, one can excel from an absolute perspective. In that case, it is *to approximate the ideal.*